Plays By
Rochelle Owens

Broadway Play Publishing Inc

New York

BroadwayPlayPub.com

Plays By Rochelle Owens
© Copyright 2000 Rochelle Owens

First printing: March 2000
I S B N: 978-0-88145-172-6

Book design: Marie Donovan
Copy editing: Michele Travis
Typeface: Palatino

CONTENTS

ABOUT THE AUTHOR

A central figure in the international avant-garde for over thirty-five years, Rochelle Owens is a playwright, poet, translator, and video artist. A pioneer of the experimental Off-Broadway theater movement, she is widely recognized as one of the most innovative and controversial writers of her generation whose groundbreaking work has influenced subsequent experimental playwrights and poets. Since its first publication in 1961, FUTZ has become a classic of the American avant-garde theatre and an international success. The play was made into a film which has itself attained the status of a cult following. Among her other works for the stage are THE STRING GAME, BECLCH, ISTANBOUL, HOMO, HE WANTS SHIH, and THE KARL MARX PLAY. She has published four collections of plays and sixteen books of poetry. Her newest books are *New And Selected Poems 1961-1996*, and *Luca: Discourse On Life & Death*. Her plays have been presented at festivals in Avignon, Berlin, Edinburgh, and Paris, and translated into French, German, Greek, Japanese, Spanish, Swedish, and Ukrainian. She has been the recipient of five *Village Voice* Obie Awards, and honors from the New York Drama Critics Circle. She has also been the recipient of grants from The Solomon R Guggenheim Foundation, The New York Creative Artists in Public Service Program, The National Endowment for the Arts, and The Rockefeller Foundation. She has taught at Brown University, the University of California-San Diego, the University of Oklahoma, and the University of Southwestern Louisiana. She has lectured and read widely in the United States and Europe.

ALSO BY ROCHELLE OWENS

Plays

FUTZ *and What Came After*
THE KARL MARX PLAY *& Others*
EMMA INSTIGATED ME
THE WIDOW & THE COLONEL
MOUNTAIN RITES
FUTZ *and* WHO DO YOU WANT, PEIRE VIDAL?

Poetry

Not Be Essence That Cannot Be
Four Young Lady Poets
Salt & Core
I Am the Babe of Joseph Stalin's Daughter
Poems from Joe's Garage
The Joe 82 Creation Poems
The Joe Chronicles Part 2
Shemuel
French Light
Constructs
W C Fields in French Light
How Much Paint Does the Painting Need
Black Chalk
Rubbed Stones and Other Poems
New and Selected Poems 1961-1996
Luca: Discourse on Life & Death

Editor

Spontaneous Combustion: Eight New American Plays

Translation

The Passersby by Liliane Atlan

Film

Futz

Video

How Much Paint Does the Painting Need
Black Chalk

Recordings

From a Shaman's Notebook
The Karl Marx Play Songs
Totally Corrupt
Black Box 17
Wild River; Light & Dust Mobile Anthology

CHUCKY'S HUNCH

CHUCKY'S HUNCH was produced by Theater for the New City (Crystal Field and George Bartenieff, artistic directors) in New York City on 22 March 1981. The cast and creative contributors were:

CHUCKY . . . . .Kevin O'Connor

Director . . . . Elinor Renfield
Sets . . . . .Abe Lubelski
Costumes . . . . Carla Kramer
Lighting . . . . .Peter Kaczorowski
Sound . . . . Paul Garrity

CHUCKY'S HUNCH reopened at the Harold Clurman Theatre in New York City on 16 February 1982.

CHARACTER

CHUCKY: *A man with graying hair wearing a turtleneck sweater and a worn shapeless tweed jacket. He is a failed artist of about fifty years old. He is sitting on a worn upholstered chair; a foot-stool is near. There is a table next to him; on it are a few random carpenter's tools, a decanter of water, and a wooden bird feeder construction.*

A NOTE CONCERNING DIRECTION

This monologue was created out of a series of never-answered letters to CHUCKY's ex-wife Elly who at times he calls by other names. CHUCKY is never in the act of writing the letters. The direction should focus on the humorous as well as the darker aspects of the inner and outer world of CHUCKY. His voice reveals anger, arrogance, contempt, cynicism, envy, glee, mockery, self-pity, spite and torment.

The play may be presented with a simplified interior setting, and a minimum of props. The director can decide whether or not to actually present CHUCKY's mother or to have a voice on tape. The musical transitions may be substituted.

CHUCKY: Okay, so you and I cut through some of those lies over twenty years ago. Beginning in 1956. That's cool. My message to you now is: Elly, who are YOU talking to? Dear Della, remember the Christmas when we hitchhiked across the country together? It was in 1958. Dig? And the young trucker asked us if we lived like that—picking up rides across the U S A. The joker was amazed, wiped out by our pre-hippy lifestyle. But he didn't know a thing about us because, and I must repeat, because we never told him our names! He who knows my name has power over me! Shit—I never wrote my name big enough for you—you refugee from Brooklyn. Ethnic! Oh, I beg your pardon, I promised myself this is going to be a polite communication. I just wanted to congratulate you for winning all that dough in the lottery, Elly. Hey, you never answered any of my other letters. What's the matter—Whatsis Face wouldn't let you? You know what I did today? I fed Freddy and the puppies. Yup. Freddy is my four-year-old husky. What a beautiful dog. He and the puppies are in the room next to Ma's room. Yup, here we are, the two of us, my eighty-five-year-old Ma and I, in her dilapidated dream house. What a stink-pit. You and Whatsis Face ought to come out and take a look. Hey, I'll even build a fire for you. Poor old Ma—little did she know that her blue-eyed boy would come to such a bad end. The old woman just lies in bed fifteen hours a day. I can't blame her—what the fuck is there to get up for? Last night I got smashed and I was stalking through the old house with a hammer in my hand. The furnace was on the blink and I was trying to fix it but I also knew that old Ma was kinda scared of me. We'd had a fight. She gets mad because she has to help support me on her Social Security checks. She says I'm just like George. You remember who he was—my father! Well, you know I never knew my father. He was no good and old American, as Ma says, and I'm an awful lot like him and she sure stresses the word "awful." But I'm an artist, remember— an abstract expressionist that is. And you're just a housewife. I have this book that I've been working on a few years now—you and Whatsis Face ought to read it. It tells the way it is and was—it even goes into the American art world scene and I like to think that it's a metaphor for the American political scene as well. You have to be a hustler to make it big. Hey, have you heard the one about the ethnic who goes to get gas? Ah, you wouldn't get the gist of it—you just wouldn't get the gist. Speakin' of ethnics—the way these Portuguese here in town treat me when I go to their goddamned one and only bar—you'd think I was the local, I don't know what—pervert! I was talking to Marie the waitress about it the other night. Boy, I'd love to get into a knock-down drag-out fight with her. Prone position—we might really make some sense together. Hey, how's Whatsis

Face? Can he hear with all the wax in his ears? That's gonna be the title
of my next book: Earwax of America's Minorities. You know, ineluctable
Della, what really grinds your jaws as well as pissing you off—is my own
failings! *C'est vrai*? It's the times. The times, dearie. My own failings are
enmeshed with the times! Is that problematic enough for you—you refugee
from Brooklyn! You... But let's not get impolite, Chucky. Nope. I'm going to
restrain myself. Be cool. Hey, Elly, you still like to munch on chicken legs?
I remember you used to like to talk about philosophical subjects when you
had a piece of chicken between your fingers. Dig? Well, again, I just wanted
to congratulate you on winning the lottery. Remember Ms Housewife—the
profit-making system never contaminated me. Sincerely, Chucky. An
American Artist.

(Lights dim. Taped music of Greensleeves *offstage.)*

CHUCKY: Dear Della-Fella,
May I call you Della-Fella? You think that's an irrelevant question, don't
you? Well, don't you? You middle-class babe in the woods. Wow! Here I
go again, and I wanted to get off on the right side of the sack with you. Dig?
All kidding aside, I spoke to our mutual friend Ronnie some weeks ago and
he said you look insane. Hey, Della-Fella, when you decided to walk out
on me twenty years ago because I was too much of an artist for the likes
of a bourgeois cunt like you really are—even though you conned a lot
of members of the ear-wax generation into believing you might be an
artist—did you ever dream that I'd end up here in this neck of the woods?
Living with my eighty-five year-old mother in a rotting pre-Revolutionary
house in a remote part of upstate New York? Hey, wow, I started my
drinking at ten this morning before I got old Ma her breakfast. Yeah, Ma
was having her bacon and eggs and Sonny-boy was taking his first snort.
Then my dog Freddy took a leak on the laundry that I brought back
spanking clean from the laundromat. Ma's gonna yell bloody murder when
she smells her sheets. And yesterday morning I went to my new employer
to ask for an advance on my salary and the mean bitch turned me down
because I already owe her fifty bucks. She told me she's going to call the
cops if I continue to bother her. Bother her? Shit! Well, fuck it! Tomorrow's
a new day and I'm going to renovate this beautiful old church in town—
I asked them if I could—incredible stained-glass windows—like the rose
window at Chartres. Remember? Sometimes I start thinking of when I was
seven years old sitting on my grandmother's porch in Michigan, holding a
glass of cold water and a chocolate nut cookie—and then I think of what Ma
always says—how did I ever get out of the mid-West alive? Anyway, back
at the ranch, guffaw, guffaw! I mean I seriously am going to renovate this
gothic-style church. Hey, why don't you ever call me up? I gave you my
phone number. Tell Whatsis Face that he's welcome to read my novel also.
Did I ever tell you that I had this beautiful parrot that could whistle and
some bastard shot him? And did I ever tell you that Sally, the girl I married

after you, DellaFella, had a baby by an East Indian and the baby's rear-end was covered with black spots? Wow! I used to be able to fuck a lot. Ha! Marie, the waitress, says I'm the only middle-aged adolescent she knows. I'm going to be fifty soon, and my teeth are rotting away. Heaven help me. Your faithful friend, Chucky. P.S. Please excuse my rudeness. I got carried away. I really would like some contact and to be able to feel like a member of the human race once again. C.C.

(Lights dim. Taped music of Italian madrigals offstage. Then, lights up.)

CHUCKY: Dear Della-Fella,
See what you made me do? Yeah, you did it, kiddo. Anybody ever tell you about yourself—like I did?—literally uncorking that dumb little housewife's mind that's stuck somewhere between your ears? Put that in your pipe and smoke it! Dig? I'm sitting here now after scolding the puppies for teasing Freddy—named after the famous and important Freddy Held who made it big in the New York art scene. Freddy Held, yeah. How could a boy like me and from the mid-West ever compete with the biggies from the city. Oops, there I go again digressing—Ma says that I'm the most digressing person she's ever seen—and she ought to know after all the times we've digressed each other. But you know my story, dear Elly. I could tell Whatsis Face much more easily than I could tell you how women have always lorded it over me. You are part of the problem. Forget the Freudian chicken soup— you refugee from Brooklyn! The trouble is I know whatever Chucky wants Chucky gets—I also know the real trouble is that Chucky doesn't always know what he wants. After you and I split up, when I was with my third wife, Sally, in 1961, I went into the antique business. Yeah, I knew that would make you laugh—but I had a little antique shop—and then everything started to fall apart—I mean the bottom of my life was starting to drop out—maybe I'm too nervous! Shucks, look what you got me doing— complaining about the conditions of my life. Now don't tell me to see a shrink because I tried it. It didn't work! I know, my perceptions at times are completely messed up. But not nearly as messed up and rotten as yours must be—No! No! No! I refuse to let you get worked up in defense of yourself! You really ought to care about what happens to your fellow human beings in this world which is part of the cosmos. You ought to because it is your responsibility to! My mother's legs are mapped all over with varicose veins and she's a dope addict. What difference does it make because she's eighty-five? Are you saying that? Well, when I look in the mirror I see someone I don't recognize who gets mad at his mother for growing too old to care anymore about her legs, or even having din-din in a little restaurant. Oh, how incorrigible I yam, I yam. Yeah. But just remember I was more intelligent than you! I WAS MORE INTELLIGENT THAN YOU! Boy, I got you worked up. This time I really got a rise outta you. Listen, between the phonies of the big shitty, yeah New York is the big shitty. Heh, heh, heh. Anyway between the phonies—I repeat the phonies of the

art world scene and you—it's a wonder that the magic christian ever got
out alive! Remember Della-Fella, if I wanted to suck seed, yeah, suck seed—
I could have—but I didn't want to. Listen dearie, drop me a line or two.
I'm sure we can communicate—maybe we can even meet in a hotel room
somewhere and finally fight it out. Remember the mosaic that I did over
twenty years ago? The knight with his lovely lady. He was playing the
lute—and she sat there next to him—with an empty smile. Your American
Artist. Charles.

(Lights dim. Taped music of jazz. Music stops. Lights up.)

CHUCKY: Dear Elly,
In spite of your winning the lottery ticket, you're a failure! You and I are
both failures. Do you dig it? And so is Ma. You know what happened to
her today? She slipped in the bathtub and fell down real hard on her ass—
she accused me of pushing her! I was only trying to help her out of the
goddamn tub! The phone company ought to be bombed like Con Edison
was in the sixties. Actually, Con Edison was never bombed, but there was
this sore loser who had a grudge and intended to bomb Con Ed. My grudge
is against the phone company. Hey, what do you think of a person who
makes crank calls? Do you think he's crazy? Do you think that individual
has a grudge against somebody? Hey, Della-Fella, how come you never
had a kid? Where have all the children gone, long time passing...?
You remember in 1958 when I was interviewed by that young twerp
from the Columbia School of Journalism and he suspected that I was
of a rebellious nature. And he told me, "We can't afford to have defiant
characters in our midst." Hey, Della, did you think that I was a defiant
character? I was really too much for you, wasn't I? From the very first day
that I met you when I told you about my life with my first wife, Hettie, you
thought of me as the sonovabitch in your life. But at least you came close to
knowing a real artist. I'm sure about certain things. In the same way that the
French Impressionists knew that the emphasis on the quality of light would
separate them from the meat and brown gravy of the traditionalist school.
From Rembrandt. It's in my book. It's all in my book. I want to send you
my book because you're in it too. It's about you, Della. The book's about
you. Do you remember my old hernia operation? The fissure that I have
on my side? It still oozes sometimes. My old hernia trouble. It sounds like
a song. God what a disgusting mess I yam, I yam. But I still get horny.
The other night I took a package of beef kidneys that were supposed to
be for the cats, yup, we have two of them running around. I let the kidneys
get at room temperature, then I wrapped them in a pair of panties and
somehow managed to work myself up into a state of sexual desire—and
came into the kidneys. Pretty depraved, right? Do you remember during the
fifties you used to wear your dark red lipstick over your lip-line, a fat round
arc that glistened—you were stacked like a brick shithouse. You were my
foot-stool, Elly. I just had an image of you eating with your head bent way

over close to the kitchen table, without your eyeglasses you were almost blind. It took guts and patience for you to get used to the contact lenses that I bought for you. Please try to show a little gratitude. Your faithful former husband, Chucky.

(Lights dim. Taped music of jazz. Music stops. Black-out.)

CHUCKY: Dear Elly,
You ole rubber hammer, you. I'm sorry for coming on strong. Forgive Chucky. It's a deal? Cool. I'll start again more politely. Dear Della. Last night Ma began her usual lecture, that is when I remove her muzzle she starts her yapping. Boy she can sure bug a man. Anyway, she began as always, stressing the two most important qualities a civilized human being must have: A sound mind in a sound body. Well, can you believe it? I have to help her in and out of the tub and wash her feet for her and she keeps up that damn song and dance about a sound mind in a sound body and how I ought to get myself together. At night, Elly, those reptile age fears come to me. Anyway, Ma and I did sit down together for a talk about the good old days when I would eat a whole head of lettuce all by myself at the age of twelve. And then the tale about the time a man tried to get into the house when Ma left me there alone. He was a genuine mid-Western pervert who probably wanted to assfuck a young boy and then cut his throat. Ma and I hugged each other real close after that story—we might have our differences but we still don't want any physical harm to come to Chucky. So what if my brain has turned to egg white. *(Lights up)* I'm still able to take a leak and make a phone call every so often. Why don't you answer, Della? What's the matter with you? Do you have cancer? How do you pay your food bills, Della? I'd like to hear you whisper in my ear and say "Hello, Chucky." I was bitten by a woman who turned into a mean green-head fly by the name of Della. Sometimes folks around here see me walking along the road with the moonlight in my hair, carrying a sawed-off shot gun. Guess who I want to find, dear woman? Peggy Guggenheim. Parasite, that's what she is— just a parasitic douche-bag. Hell, I'll never send her one of my bird-feeder constructions. Nope, Peggy's never gonna get a bird-feeder from Chucky. Only lucky Della-Fella will. Dig? I should answer my back door, the handy-man wants to talk about a leaking roof. He's ringing away and Ma's screaming bloody murder because I won't let him in the house. She thinks I was traumatized by the memory of the pervert from years back. Traumatized? Me. Never! The only thing that ever really got me down was the suicides of all our friends. Especially our dear mutual friend, Eugene Ruggles. Well, you can be sure his wife never knew Genie's whereabouts that night. My, oh my, don't I sound like some suburban housewife? I don't mean to be rude, of course, of course. I introduced you to the music of Bach, never forget that kid, you ole rat, you. You were just an unformed baby when I met you. I created you—you Frankenstein monster! Now, I'm the only one who listens to me. I'm a troubador poet. What a fucking place

America is. I should have won a Prix de Rome or a Guggenheim. The handy-man is banging away like a crazy-man and Ma's screaming at me to let him in, but I won't. Chucky is not taking any chances, at least not yet. When I answer the door I'm going to have a brick in my hand. How about you, Della, do you keep a brick in your hand when the doorbell rings? Chucky.

(*Lights dim. Taped music of Elvis Presley,* Blue Suede Shoes. *Music stops.*)

CHUCKY: Dear Lying Eyes,
How's that for a title of a book I'm going to write? "Dear Lying Eyes." You know the trouble with you is you won't answer any of my letters. What's the matter—are your fingers too greasy to hold a pen? I bet you've become a woman's libber since I went out of your life, Della. But we can always talk about it if you want in some low-down hotel room. How's about it, Della? I'm great at pre-chewing food if that's what you need. No kidding, I can chew your food for you. I do it for Ma. Yup, the woman's bridge broke last week because I accidentally smacked her in the mouth with my big carpenter's hand and so I thought that I ought to help her eat by chewing the goddamn food for her so that she can get some nourishment in her. And there's more of an emotional connection chewing up the food than using an automatic blender. Eskimo mothers do it for their kids, I thought I'd try it. How's that for a boy's devotion? Ma doesn't mind. She just looks at me while swallowing what Chucky gives her. I just remembered a little incident years and years ago, in 1960. You and I were strolling along in the Village one sweet summer night, heading for the San Remo, and a bum asked me for some change and for one reason or another, probably because the sonovabitch was too aggressive, I didn't give him anything and he got bittershit and bawled at our backs as we meandered on our way—"You got a woman! You got a woman!" Talk about middle-class values. The fucker thought I should give him some money because I had a woman. Don't put me down, Della. I can still show you a thing or two. The magic christian is still as beautiful as Michelangelo's David. Ma showed me a recipe for chili. I'm going to try it tomorrow. When I put my mind to it I can do anything. After all the suffering Ma has had in her life, to think that her only child, her son, would end up this way. But here I am going off again like a roach out of a crack in the wall. I should cut out the cigarettes, it's making what teeth I have left a very obnoxious green. You used to have strong teeth, Della, big like a horse's. I can visualize you with your big teeth, smiling broadly at me, laughing your head off the way you always did whenever you became nervous. You were so nervous when I knew you. This is for you, Della-Fella. Ma has a bad cough that's not getting better. She insists on smoking up a storm. It's a wonder that she hasn't died of T.B. or cancer. Hah! She'll probably outlive me. Women with their sexual organs are the stronger sex. Dig? I'm pretty sure Ma still gets horny. I know what I'm talking about. And me? I feel like I'm doing myself in but I don't want to do this shitty

world any favors—not just yet anyway. Your immortal artist, Charles Craydon. P S Elly, when you left me over twenty years ago I bet that you took the big hand-knit Christmas stocking that Ma made to remind you of the old days. I'd like to fill that stocking up with oranges and bars of chocolate and best wishes from your good fairy, Chucky.

(Lights dim. Taped voice resembling that of a news broadcaster.)

TAPED VOICE: The snake and the porcupine had been a couple for five years. Spawned in the woods near Apple Valley, New York, they were a symbiotic entity, cunning, vicious, frightening, above all pragmatic during a killing. In judging this unique duo who liked to play games in the moist muddy furrows near the pond, one had to understand and accept the fantastic attraction the two had for each other; it was something special, ever since the members of their different species had rejected and thrown them out of the home territory for obscure reasons that affront and mock those who hold to current scientific opinion about the unlikelihood of wild animals from different genres forming alliances. This was an extraordinary pair, intelligent and prospering. During that first incredible encounter, the porcupine had dropped seventeen quills to the earth in fright because she had believed that the snake was going to sting her to death. He wanted only to touch her where there were no quills, to rub his length along her voluptuous roundness. With inscrutable thoroughness they smelled each other ravenously. The seasons sailed by and each and every spring struck them as some new wonder of the senses that they had never known before. Together they were rich and glorious, mating, mating always, gasping and hissing in an attempt to beget progeny, meeting each other's opaque gaze in their mutual trance of copulation. The snake and the porcupine did not fear man as the members of their respective species did, although they knew that man caused trouble to the creatures that lived in their midst. There is no more reason to give credence to one theory than to the other—as to why they didn't fear humans, or why they became a couple. One of the most dramatic fights that they had shared together was when they had seized a large husky and began to chew its head and neck so violently that the victim thrashed about wildly in an effort to escape. After the struggling had ended, the pair spent an hour swallowing their prey. All the while a man watched from a nearby bush, showing curiosity and agitation. When the pair made especially violent movements he dashed away in terror only to return again to peer through the bush at the fascinating spectacle. After the meal the couple did a slipping and skidding and zigzagging dance that slowly progressed into copulation.

(Taped music: West Indian Steel Guitars.)

CHUCKY: Dear Elly,
I think that yours truly got a bum rap. Not only is Ma complaining more loudly than usual about how bad it is to be old without any grandchildren

to make jam and bake cookies for, but also that her very own magic christian son is such a god-awful loser. Yup, one of life's real losers, I yam, I yam. The saddest thing I have to report to you is that my husky, a great big gorgeous animal, kind of like I was when I was twenty, my Freddy, was murdered and eaten in cold blood by the weirdest twosome I've ever seen collaborating in a killing. Yup. A snake and a porcupine ganged up on Freddy my dog and killed him. I saw it with my own eyes. I bet you're thinking why didn't I scare them off by throwing a rock or something—because my hernia was acting up and I felt awful. And I was in much too weak a condition to defend myself. Anyway, I cried like a baby all night thinking about what happened to my husky.

Ma couldn't say a word to me without my biting her head off. See, I blame her for my hernia because of the Jehovah Witness phase that she went through when I was fifteen, that forbade her to allow me to undergo surgery for my hernia. A simple operation then could have cured me of the damn thing, but Ma's religious scruples prevented me from having it. Is it any wonder that I suffer emotionally as well as sometimes oozing from the fissure in my side from the operation I was forced to have later? Ma's been having grimy thoughts lately—been confiding to me how she has sexual urges and at her age. Eighty-five, God bless her. Says that if only she could meet some nice gentleman at a church social. She begs me to take her to church when she's feeling perky some Sundays. But why should I please her when she wouldn't let me have the hernia operation when I was fifteen? That year when the other boys in the locker room at school found out about my wearing a truss. She could have spared me the pain and embarrassment of the boys' ridicule. I originally wanted to tell you about my dog Freddy's death but I got sidetracked as usual. But do you know any old man who might like to get it on with my mom? He doesn't even have to be a White Anglo-Saxon Protestant. But, I'd better check out her preference first.

Ma's still choosy even after having given birth to a snake-in-the-grass like Chucky. Somehow I always felt that I deserved a better name than loser in my life. I mean I had more options than you twenty years ago. I was the one with the superior intelligence and the physical strength. I was the artist and you were just a pretender. But then the female spider does devour the male. Right rubber hammer? How many men have you chewed up, you fat spider? Sign off, bug off, fuck off, jerk off. Chucky.

(Lights dim. Taped music of Stormy Weather)

CHUCKY: Dear Lost Wonder,
I'm in a slightly gentler state of mind today. Ma did it! Yup. She's got a companion, a boyfriend. No, I'm not kidding. It's true as pimples on a teenaged girl's derriere. Remember when I told you about Ma wanting a male friend who she could ha, ha, relate to? You know what I mean, Elly, somebody who she could rub her muddy ole body on and maybe chew a thumb or two. Anyway, lemme tell thee what's transpired since. Gee, I feel

like I'm telling a fragment of a medieval saga. Here goes. Last Sunday morning, when I went back to the house after dropping Ma off at church, there was a fog over the pond, what some of the older people around here used to call Jack-in-the-mist. All of a sudden something flashed in my brain. It came to me that something extraordinary was happening that exact moment to Ma right in church. I had this feeling that Ma was very happy at that very moment. Oh, I've had these hunches before. When we were married, I had a hunch the day after we exchanged vows that you were going to leave me. You did leave me too. You cunt. You couldn't stand the fact of being married to an artist. But it's cool. I forgive you kid. Shit I'm digressing from my story about Ma and the old man who maybe I'll be calling Pop one of these days. His name is Chester Nickerson and he's eighty-two years-old, but if he told you he was sixty-five you'd believe the son-of-a-gun. He's a retired gentleman, to use Ma's words, and he has several children and nine grandchildren, also a nephew who publishes a national magazine. Ma is much happier now that she's found Chester and to tell you the truth, I'm trying to share her happiness. You should see her when she's preparing tea for the two of them, Ma calls it high tea because she serves crumpets in the English manner. She asks me to join them but I know when I'm not wanted—the old bugger is trying to get into Ma's pants. Heh, heh—so I just wander off and leave the two of them alone, but my imagination starts to work overtime and I feel terribly confused because I know Ma doesn't have too many years left and her legs are bad, the old man couldn't care less about Ma's legs looking like broken sausages or all the medication she takes that I'm sure makes her feel horny. Geezus! My brain is popping with pictures, hey, that's a good expression, isn't it? Yeah, my brain is popping with pictures of Ma and Chester Nickerson getting it off together. I know what you're thinking—that they couldn't possibly be making it at their age but that's not true, a person could keep having sex until deep into old age. Why, I expect to make it with room-temperature beef kidneys until I'm fifty-five. Why fifty-five? Because frankly I don't know how much longer I can go on this way, being drunk almost every day, my inability to hold down a job and the affections of my beloved Ma being stolen from me by this dirty old man called Chester Nickerson. And last, but not least, the murder of my dog Freddy. God I miss him so. In a way Freddy was just like a little child, my son, and Ma's grandchild. Don't laugh at my sadness, Elly. God will judge you. Your faithful, Chucky.

(Lights dim. Taped music of tango.)

CHUCKY: Dear Della,
What is happening to me right now is like out of an X-rated film; I'm sure of it as I'm sure of my own name "Chucky Craydon." But it's the circumstances of my life, and Ma and Chester Nickerson, her eighty-two-year-old lover. Yup. It happened yesterday morning when he arrived at the house with his flowers for another one of his long chats with Ma. I decided

to join them at tea. During their conversation about politics
he began to look in my direction, a kind of weird stare, and then he'd look
at Ma and I could see at once that there was an alliance between them
against me. Then out of the blue he announces that the speedometer on
his car reads exactly 69,696.9 miles and that was a good number to dwell
on and then after saying this nutty statement Ma looks at me with her chin
trembling a little and tells me why don't I go into town for the newspaper.
I had already made a trip to the dump and I felt like lounging around a little
in my own home! Dig? Yes, I know the house is in Ma's name but after her
death it's mine! But the way my blood pressure is these days because of all
the aggravation I'll probably go first. Anyway, to get back to the point, I tell
the both of them that I know they want to be alone and I'll leave to do some
work on my new bird-feeder constructions that I've been making. You
ought to see them Elly, they're beautiful. Well, I worked a half hour on
the bird-feeder constructions and then I thought I'd just slip around to the
back of the house outside Ma's bedroom where she and Chester Nickerson
are and I'm peering through the gap between the window shade and the
sill and I see that Chester is in the middle of sticking the pink and purple
wildflowers that he likes to bring to Ma into her bun on the nape of her neck
and Ma is laughing and fiddling around with the zipper of his fly, pulling it
up and down in a playful way and then Ma puts her hand all the way in so
that it appears that the hand is cut off at the wrist and Chester is sticking his
tongue into Ma's ear and then Chester stands up and drops his pants and
while still in his boxer shorts that are almost to his knees he pulls up Ma's
flowered housedress so that she's sort of trapped temporarily in the
armholes and then Chester is unlacing Ma's corset and her breasts which
still look, I swear Elly, almost like a woman in her forties, were free for
Chester to fondle. I was stunned! I could hardly believe my own eyes when
I saw what went on between them. Ma sucking Chester's soft gray dick
until it grew hard and then Ma sitting right smack on Chester's face, pulling
at his hands with her arthritic fingers, clutching at his wrists while making
low groans in the back of her throat. I admit that though I was jealous
at what those two had between them, I was also furious and I just hoped
Ma wouldn't die of heart failure, or for that matter, Chester. I almost burst
out laughing when I saw Ma stick the rim of a small vial of perfume into
Chester's asshole. Where on earth did Ma learn her techniques? I wonder
that sometimes. They started to fuck with Ma on the edge of the bed and
Chester standing in front of her. By that time the noise of their gasping was
beginning to sound terribly loud and scary in my own ears and my anxiety
was becoming more than I could bear and all I could think of was a glass of
cold water and a chocolate nut cookie and being seven years old again. But
then I had an image of burning the house down with them inside. And all I
wanted really was to get very drunk and be with my dog Freddy who I miss
more than this world can ever know. We gave away the puppies and now
all I have left is the memory of Freddy. My mother wishes I were dead so

that she and Chester Nickerson can be alone together for their remaining years. The feeling around my heart is one of constant pain. The booze offers me some relief but it's all false, just like the values of this world are. Well, I intend to avenge the death of Freddy. I'm going to find and hunt down the deadly duo that took his life. Soon, my quest begins. Until later, Chucky. P.S. Did you know that Ma got a job a month ago stuffing envelopes and I think she's made about a thousand dollars from an outfit in Daytona Beach, Florida. But I haven't seen one red cent of it. Still another reason that feeds my anger against Chester Nickerson—I bet she gives him the money.

(Lights up. CHUCKY is sleeping, head folded in arms. He awakens and sits looking out at audience. Face in shadow. A very deep woman's voice offstage. Taped)

WOMAN'S VOICE: Dear Elly,
It has been so many years since any sort of correspondence between us, although I did write you a letter about seven years ago which was returned to me for reasons of change of address. Luckily, I was able to get your present whereabouts from the newspapers. I am very happy for you, Elly, that you had a winning ticket in the lottery. Chucky had mentioned it to me, the fact of your luck. This letter that I am in the midst of writing contains some important information that I think you ought to know. My son Chucky has disappeared and there are no available answers to where he has gone or if he is even alive this very day. I know that the fact that you were married to him so many years ago, over twenty to be exact, might lead you to the conclusion that this unhappy circumstance is not your concern, the unhappy circumstance being the disappearance. If you can't follow my line of reasoning, it is because there is no rhyme or reason or constant, orderly line to human life without spiritual convictions. Those smart alecks who are against prayer in the schools are in the upper echelons of the communist party. Anyway back to the premise of my letter and the nitty gritty facts—about two weeks ago Chucky took off about eleven in the morning, it was a Wednesday, to go to the town dump for obvious reasons of refuse removal. We had a huge load of *Readers' Digests* and old *Life* magazines dating back to the early fifties, but Chucky couldn't stand the sight of the piles of magazines and papers. I'm certain he got that impatient streak from his father George plus his predilection for drinking. At any rate, since July fifth we have not seen hide nor hair of him. Needless to say I miss my boy very much and lately my mind is filled with memories that only an old woman's mind can be filled with. Memories of when I was a young mother-to-be. I remember distinctly the desire to have a normal child and so I made sure that as soon as I found out I was pregnant, I would never wear a tight leather belt again that pressed my waist in; now I know, Elly, you always wore tight belts and I'm sure that is why you lost your baby when you were married to Chucky. But these days I think it was definitely a good thing that Chucky never had a child because I'm convinced that the reason for his terrible disturbances are due to the bad genes that he inherited from

his father George whom I had to leave because I knew that he would be dangerous to Chucky sooner or later. Oh, I was both mother and father to Chucky as you so well know and as you so well know I would if I had to have gone down on my hands and knees to scrub floors for his college education—fortunately I had a good job as an occupational therapist. I sometimes wonder when I look at the old photograph album of Chucky when he was a child, there are so many pictures of him and me together, why did the misfortunes happen to us? Not you, Elly, you've been doing well over the years. Oh, I know everybody has their troubles but Chucky had a college education. He was such a handsome young man with his dreams about being an artist. Last week was my birthday and Chucky's too. It was a miraculous coincidence that my boy and I were born on the same date. My birthday was pleasant though, I was fortunate to have spent the day with a kind and good friend who I met at church some time ago. A gentleman by the name of Chester Nickerson. He is a widower and is quite serious about remarrying. Chester is eighty-two and in perfect health. We are both of the same Protestant denomination and so forth. He has a whole lot of youthful ideas and can show a man much younger than himself a thing or two about romancing a woman. Chester has a nephew who is a publisher of a nationally known magazine and it is also sold in Europe. They have a fold-out page in each issue and Chester thinks it would be the cat's meow if photos of both him and me were taken in some elegantly refined poses displaying natural love. Of course he's joking but who knows, I cannot see the harm in decent photos of us together. Oh, dear me! I must tell you this information about Chucky's disappearance instead of getting sidetracked as I am apt to do—several days after Chucky's dog Freddy was killed, supposedly by a snake and a porcupine, Chucky kept talking on and on about how he was going to get the "deadly duo" who had taken the life of Freddy. The police and Chester and I theorize that he probably decided to try to find and hunt down the alleged killers of Freddy. They have even put bloodhounds on his trail but have come up with nothing. I'm worried sick over the whole business of Chucky but I've still got to think of practical affairs, like contacting the town refuse dumping-service to come and collect my garbage once a week. Chucky used to do that for us—load up all the refuse in the car and take it to the dump. When he'd return I'd always ask him about the magpies and how many there were that day lunching at the dump. The idea of all those birds eating there at the dump just tickled me. Well, I must sign off now. I hope that you are enjoying yourself this summer. Sincerely yours, Marge Craydon. P S. There was a special prayer service for Chucky offered up by the congregation of the church last Sunday. How I hope all our prayers will be answered and that he will return home safe and sound. Because no corpse has been discovered the police have given up the search and have come to believe that he might have left the area.

(Lights dim. Taped Japanese non-vocal music. Lights up.)

CHUCKY: Dear Snap-hole, Della-Fella,
If you took a poll and you dressed up in a black suit, a man's suit that is, you could call yourself Mr Death. Because like I've told you before and in so many ways—you know all the answers, Elly. So then tell me how I ever found myself in this neck o' the woods. Listen to me, Elly, and like Ishmael I'm going to relate a tale to ye in as high-pitched a decibel as I can make— but like a bat or a porpoise you'll be able to understand what the fuck's been happening to yours truly these past few weeks. For example—what actually was I doing lurking around unfamiliar territory in the first place? Sure I was hunting down the murderers of Freddy—that was my objective. But did I ever consider that I might have experienced an extraordinary phenomenon—and not any mystical bullshit either. Oh come on, Elly, you know what I mean. Don't laugh, I feel—innocent! Yeah, innocent but still the same old nose-thumber as I always have been—and still subject to sexual impulses of a highly erotic nature. Like right now, I'm visualizing you, Elly, wearing high spike heels, your face flushed, erected nipples peeking through your fuzzy angora sweater. Do you know that there are creatures evolving this very second from out of the forest primeval, rodent-like and five-toed with long thick tails, descendants of the saber-toothed tiger? Elly, did you know that Queen Elizabeth the first had a neck shaped like an otter? Oh, if I could only show you all the different and subtle colors of a sea-slug and a squid—then you'd know that I'm still very much an artist. You might think otherwise—that I'm a lunatic. But if I'm a lunatic, Elly, then the president of the United States is a nameless hybrid, a pile of mouse turd. The way the government is treating the people—I'm amazed that the masses haven't risen up in armed revolt! I sound like a communist, don't I? You know, Elly, during the McCarthy era—I helped petition against the asshole. Ah, that's another story. Sometimes, I feel like I've been around since the birth of Christ. At this moment I'm gazing at my sharpened ax, it gleams in the moonlight—in a little while I'm going to follow the scent that keeps drifting to my nostrils, the scent of cotton-tailed rabbit and squirrel which is what I nurture my body on these days, plus some cheap whiskey that I'm able to steal from some hippy now and then. There's a Holiday Inn not too far from where I am and you can't imagine the things they put in the garbage. It makes you wonder about the kind of people at a Holiday Inn. At night while prowling around I'm aware of tremendous energy, it's during the day that I'm ravaged and exhausted in body and soul—where everywhere I stand is enemy territory—when I flail at the air and let regret wash over me like mud from the river. But Elly, I'm as curious as ever, more curious than a cat or a puppy and for complex reasons these parts of upstate New York fascinate me and there are nights when my wanderings have a clear and urgent purpose as if I'm going to find something or someone that is necessary to the continuation of my being. Your friend, Chucky.

(Taped Japanese non-vocal music.)

CHUCKY: Dear Above Average Woman,
Yeah, you are—you know it too. You like the idea also. Being above
average. Guess where I am? I'm here under the rocks with the bugs—being
watched by the dragons and owls of hysterical imagination. Elly, if I've seen
a weird thing—I mean something really weird—I might just chalk it up to
being loaded or whatever, but if I see the weird thing again and again, well
then I possibly might be correct in my perceptions. Right? Right. You know
about the Holiday Inn, well, there are some very peculiar goings-on there.
Shit—I want to tell it exactly how I remember. One twilight after I had
rescued a nest full of birds from a coupla cats—I heard a din coming from
the swimming pool at the Holiday Inn—so I took a look and it turned out
to be a gaggle of kids of about twelve—they were riding bicycles around
in circles—horsing round the way kids do. I noticed a very lively one who
had make-up on his eyes and a leather studded wrist band. He was really
a handsome kid. You know a guy like me could really get close to a kid like
that. Get your mind out of the gutter, Elly. You know that's not my scene.
Anyway, I wanted to run off with the tyke and teach him the ways of an
Indian scout—to be silent for hours on end and wait for the fish to bite. And
then I saw the kid's father, a bearded guy who wore funny leather pouches
snapped to his belt. He was with a dwarf who was wearing yellow loafers.
All of a sudden I hear a voice yelling, "Laszlo," and the dwarf turns his big
head to look up toward the balcony where the voice is coming from. And
standing up on the balcony is an old man—and it's none other than Chester
Nickerson. Well, you can imagine what I was feeling at that moment, Elly.
But that wasn't the biggest surprise. Oh, no. Because I saw my mom step
out on the balcony and she was holding a tall glass of what could have been
vodka and tonic and she was wearing a red and yellow gown, and she was
smiling. She looked terrific, Elly. I felt my armpits begin to itch. I controlled
myself and refrained from screaming bloody murder. Then I see Ma rest
her hand on the back of Chester's neck and then he turned to kiss her wrist.
I felt as if someone had poured concrete down my throat. I couldn't stand
it another minute. I ran away from the Holiday Inn. I went deep into the
woods. I felt so wrong in the scheme of things. Do you know, Elly, that the
sun is my enemy—a great ball of fire that pours out its hate. I need a colder
climate like the Arctic tundra. I used to wonder why the bloodhounds
hadn't picked up my scent. I used to wonder that—but now I know. I'm
wasted—and the dogs have given up on me. Elly, it's true. And you're so
fucking indestructible! Well, I've got news for you—I intend to inherit my
piece of the earth. The Rebel, Charles Craydon.

(Lights dim. Taped music of Italian madrigals. Time passes.)

CHUCKY: Elly,
I have an image of you in my mind, poking like a finger under my eyelids.
You're standing next to a vase filled with wildflowers. My ego is growing
claws that are ready to tear off a piece of whatever I can get them into. There

is no pattern to my life that you can understand, Elly. I have a hunch, you'll find yourself basking in the sun with me one of these days—but the odds are against it. You'll most likely die in a mental institution at a ripe old age. What do you think of when you look at the old photographs of us together? Do you feel as though you walked away from a head-on collision? I talk to you—you refuse to understand. I loved the way you moved your body—and not once have I pitched woo with anyone but you, dear.

(Lights down slowly.)

END OF PLAY

FUTZ

FUTZ was first presented for one performance on 10 October 1965, at the Tyrone Guthrie Workshop at the Minnesota Theater Company.

FUTZ was then presented by the LaMama Troupe on 1 March 1967, at The LaMama Experimental Theater Club in New York City. The cast and creative contributors were:

NARRATOR	Beverly Atkinson
CYRUS FUTZ	John Bakos
MAJORIE SATZ	Beth Porter
OSCAR LOOP	Seth Allen
BILL MARJORAM	Michael Warren Powell
KEEPER	Peter Craig
ANN FOX	Mari-Claire Charba
SHERIFF TOM SLUCK	Peter Craig
FATHER SATZ	Rob Thirkield
MOTHER SATZ	Mari-Claire Charba
BROTHER NED SATZ	Victor LiPari
MRS LOOP	Marilyn Roberts
WARDEN	Peter Craig
SUGFORD	Michael Warren Powell
BUFORD	Peter Craig

Music & direction	Tom O'Horgan
Set design	Saito
Lighting	Laura Rambaldi
Technical assistance	Howard Vishinsky

AUTHOR'S NOTES

The various settings of the play may be simply suggested with a minimum of props. The techniques of film, especially montage, quick-cutting, lighting, and musical backup, should be utilized. It is important that the director keep in mind the dynamics of rhythm, imagery, and tonal meanings within the language. The actor has worlds within worlds to play. The elements of humor ought to be found so that the darker aspects emerge with stronger impact.

Except for the characters CYRUS FUTZ, MAJORIE SATZ, and OSCAR LOOP, the actors can double in the other roles.

Now concerning the things whereof ye wrote unto me:
It is good for a man not to touch a woman.

1 Corinthians 7:1

Scene One

NARRATOR: Let's give it a strange passion to a story, some handyman handy in the barns with animals—"someone to watch over him"—somethings, the udders of the moo-moo especially. No stupid pretty girl to rely on him, like a homemade stunt between his feet, to knock up his knees—bad onions—spoiling him eternally. Small fetid room, obvious barn-like, but still a small room with lots of oily automobile rags and other signs of the terrible city existence, brewed still more stinky with the worst the country has to offer—dead grassy worms, horses' shit, small portions of a moldy outhouse, summer brooms, women's drawers, rubber suits for working in the water, etc. Anything you can think up naturally. Cy Futz, a Scandinavian sort of big fellow, wearing new dungarees, bell bottom, they could be overalls, comes in filled with a sexual dream; it does not bear in the least to anything real in terms of yours or Cy's world. It's pure sickness, but in its pureness it's a truth. Sitting down on a wet broken step, he says:

CY: O the cow's tits are bigger and I know it's wrong, but young uns never know the difference between an animal's or a woman's hip bones, so soft like my socks, fresh washed like new kid's hoofs. O I could sing. OOOOOoooOOOOOooooo OOOO LooLoooooooooLOOOOOOO Looy LOOY LOY LORD LORD I LOVE YOU GOD. And I have no hate for anybody, but wanting to love the animals the way I do. *They*, mean folks hate my face. I turn around the corners and make fun on their asses, no tickle does theirs feel like my own good one as I sing tears in the sow's belly. With their fried eggs for wives, they know no song.

NARRATOR: Again he sings his OOOs and looooo's intermingled with a belch and a mock fart and ending with three very loud "Lords." All the time he's buttering his wrists with his red hands, making bird and other noises, he is very excited and seems absolutely certain to explode all his love or whatever over the world which is the room where he is in now. Now she comes in, Miss Majorie Satz, about twenty-seven years old, tall with a square worldly, insulted once maybe, body. Her coarse red hair is combed up in a sophisticated way which is sweetly silly in retrospect to her ood-stained gingham, typical farm girl getup.

MAJORIE: Hello Bastady man. Yus big man-bloke, I missed you at the greengrocer, yus said that you would come, yus said so, and I painted my big toe too for yu. (*Giggling*) Yu man-bloke, old Swede man.

NARRATOR: Cyrus is looking at her and is vexed at her, probably Cy was always squinnied by her, probably because she obviously is a woman in the

very dreamy sensual way which he only wants his animals to be. Gentle
sick man he is. He hoots at her.

CY: Hallas Majy Ya French dancer! You woman of ten foot beds and manure
heaps, yus stinking human woman with only cat-mouths for tits and a
baby-paw for your arse. I did not want to see you, you told me a foul story
the last time that I saw you. Not again mind you do I want that shit! Always
you are pretending to be my friend and better yet a hole for me to dive in,
but I'd rather sink my pick in turd, cleaner my Lord more than you Maj!
Nahhh! I don't want no sow with two feet but with four! Them repeats
true things with their grunts not like you human-daughter.

NARRATOR: Majorie moves backwards and starts to hum the French anthem.

MAJORIE: I'll pick up my skirt right now if yu want. I'll get on my heels
and elbows, old farmer, yus not so old yu know only forty, there are whut's
younger men than yu who'd like to take me to a movie, strongir and
slimmir than yu, so why make me hurt your chest—an' don't I buy you
fodder for your sick love, Amanda the sow, so she could be a better one for
yu? Even I know, who likes yu, how bud it is to sleep with a pig! Unnatural,
like in the Bible, it's piggish—that's where the word comes from yus know
piggish—from a pig yugh yugh sooo evil. Yu smell so baad it is no joke—

CY: Go forget about it and your cheeks won't be nervous—put your nose
out of my business, disgusting girl. I like Amanda because she's good.
Pig or not. And I don't stink that's your lie—any much more than you
or the boys that take you in the fields.

MAJORIE: *(Hatefully)* That's your awn dirtty story 'nd it maks me nasty
towards yu—I can't feel bad for your dread and doom—yu sleep with
the unimals bitter bitter unholy unholy.

NARRATOR: Cy pushes her from behind, then stoops and picks up a dirty
broom, begins to sweep her flanks with a mock lust, also singing a very
low song in a Celtic tune. She covers her ears and shreiks.

MAJORIE: Yeeeiiiiey Oyu Big man-bloke!

NARRATOR: He snaps her rope belt with his left hand and slaps her face
*(Not hard. [Directions are either performed by the actors or verbalized by the
narrator. This is left to the decision of the director.])* with the right. He pushes
her ahead of him and they both go behind the half-rotten wall which was
once an old outhouse.

(Animal grunts sound and the lights are dimmed.)

Scene Two

NARRATOR: Look at the old rotten wall—behind it, here are Cyrus and Maj and yugch! a sow. Amanda! The animal that's sure to steal forever Cy's heart (never to marry) yus, her, Maj, sweet flower, woman with a wholesome grin, and no hair on the chin, sallow woman with a cantaloupe seed in her belly and toes that are canary yellow. Ooopph. *(He pushes his hands in a cup form and feeds the sounds of grunts and human voice to the audience.)*

MAJORIE: Pechhh *so* indecent, I'd live in shame if the village ever knew what I'd done.

CY: Fahhh my woman the people need never know what you done, anyways they would want the full freedom to be able to do what you done. Girl, peachy sweet currant stop being afraid, even the sow won't tell!

NARRATOR: Maj tears, she's sore afraid.

MAJORIE: Yu make it wus tan it is mentionin' the pig—she does not know anyting about it, and she did not feel soft like you said but like an old razor on my feet. O o o so indecent I am, and now the filty dreams 'ill come. O Gods help meee that we shoulda both laid with a sow.

NARRATOR: Maj carries about awhile with hands scratching out her Lord from the sky, pushing him into her soul, trying to wring his sweat from the skinny body, trying hard hard to have his water wash the dinny sin from her wretched body. Lust for animals is like a run in spring rain. *(Sniggle)* Lewd lewd, foosh foosh, and she calls on all the idols and the true god to make the slop go away.

CY: Now fish stop, stop fish, nobody knows and the pig won't tell.

MAJORIE: Stop stop stop! Yus mean rat, your modern sin has killed me!

CY: Isn't no modern sin, old as your Bible, lay down with a calf somebody did and did get no punishment from God, like your village will give you. Cluck, if you don't stop your sirens blowing, shit your mouth up Majorie, you're makin' me sound funny in my own ears and I have faith for my love of the animals with hoofs and corncob appitite, can't you really see—it is no wrong. They laugh more real than the mayor and your mother. Brooey to the devil for the bad conscience you feel, say phat phat to it. It don't pay.

MAJORIE: Your diggnitty is like sloppy ole shoes, but good luck to me, soon as I get away from evil—never again. Os Os never agin piggiying myself like that.

NARRATOR: She gets up from the bed of wet paper and rags, smoothing her clothes and wrapping her hair in her fists. Cy watches her with pickles in his eyes. He spys the pig and on the knees and hands jerks towards her, sticking his fingers out like stone worms, his tongue lolls like mice in his mouth, he sticks his leg out, banging his shoe on the pig's ass (not cruelly though) just enough to make the animal turn and be conscious of him, for in that white-flesh no-blood brain she remembers pleasure. And she backs towards him you know and he grabs her body. Maj is watching with bloody senses, then tears out shrieking.

Scene Three

NARRATOR: In an old-fashioned prison cell with the traditional water pot, hammock, etc., two men are talking (O everything is the same with these two as with a hundred other yolts). The jailbird, Oscar Loop, is skinny and wears the prison suit like he was a fallen priest, the other man is Bill Marjoram, squat, strong, sweaty and typical in work clothes, fat shoes, etc, how can well I go describing on?

LOOP: O breadfast is not much, I mean breakfast is not much, two pieces of bread, glass of water and a sausage, not real you know, something to think about anyway, sometimes I think like a motherless child, I mean take the tiny spices out of the sausage and grow them like small insects, I mean if they get watered and sun on them they might get life and then they'd be like insects.

BILL: Shut up, Loop! Stupid, talking 'bout insex and maybe hanging tomorra! Your riddles too! Make me sick.

LOOP: Listen, they would be spice insects, so you could eat them—they would even be medicinal, cure a palsy helpfully, jerk a dead newborn back to life. O I hope it would do all those things.

BILL: Shut up, Loop! I said. Stupid. Don't you know you gonna die?

LOOP: I mean a dead newborn could have been Mozart—I care in a great many ways for life, that's why the good sausage seed-spice might work (Whispers) without the evil eye, I bet Siva would help me, Siva is beautiful with her lovely hands, she's picked the mosquitoes out of my head. I've read greatly about her.

BILL: You keep blabbing on 'nd on 'bout things that don't stop you from dying!

LOOP: How do you know? What makes you be so sure? Anything cun help a man maybe, a rock hit a devil in the Bibledays and a devil sucked out the blood of the thrower of that rock in hell. Somebody made that devil draw out all the blood in the man. Hmmmmmmmmmmmmmmmmm I'll have to write that on the sausage. Mustn't forgit all the marvelous thoughts I git lately.

BILL: Mavilous thoughts my foot! Swear you're gonna hang on Monday. Man, think, Loop! Think! Whut did you do?

LOOP: Whut did I do? Flah! A woman saw me, she bought me a mitten, tole me to put it on, said that the feeling would come through better. She looked like Mary in a story, but not the Lord's mother you know. No she looked like the whore. But then like him I changed her.

BILL: Whut do you mean, changed her! Speak it up truthfully. You killed her!

LOOP: I made her fall asleep on the ground. Put a bad blueberry in her mouth, Satan was a grub, and when he got inside of her he ate her innards out but that was God's wish.

NARRATOR: Loop is smiling like a good king.

BILL: How did she die? And if it's too bad a story, you bitter not tell it in your crazy way. Tell me how you killed the girl, nobody dies with fruitbugs, tell it sound and real.

NARRATOR: Now there are keys and chains sounds, the prison keeper comes in and Loop, eyes frightened, begins to stretch. He is afraid that he has been heard.

(Everybody cringes.)

LOOP: I mean to say that what I tole Bill wasn't all so. *(Points to the keeper and ropes his arm toward himself.)* You come here, guard, O I'm gonna tell you how I killed the girl, but in the beginning. Hoos! In the beginning was purity, and cleanliness was a big garter belt.

NARRATOR: The keeper is sniffing in his giggles, feeling his bone, trying to see garter belts.

KEEPER: Tell us what happened and maybe you can get a reprieve, hhah ha ha ha hiss—Did you put the garter belt 'round her small throat?

LOOP: I met Ann Fox in the greengrocer's. I saw her skirt swing frisky, and I knew that her father was a good farmer and Baptist. I knew that everybody in the village liked that family. And no young fella would treat her disrespectfully. I could not just get married to a girl, without her being like Ann, I knew that I wouldn't get married and be normal—so I asked her out, and she went with me, she said she liked the smell of leather. You know I have a good leather belt and jacket that a handcrafts woman sent me. Well Ann liked that jacket, she said she'd take it from me when I was asleep. Sometimes I think she meant it too. Her father was a rich man, he could buy her all the leather clothes she wanted but she'd say she wanted my jacket too. Well I'd get mad thinking about it, though I knew too that she was playing. But I took her one night near the field where Cy Futz's barn is and we horseplayed a little bit, nothing but some hunky-punk.

Scene Four

NARRATOR: A small dark field, nighttime, a blanket on the grass, a leather jacket spread perfectly out. Oscar Loop and Ann Fox are sitting opposite each other cross-legged.

LOOP: Little good cat, ooph you knock my eyes out of my head, you're so pretty.

NARRATOR: He sticks out his forefinger and strokes her nose.

ANN: Buford Skark says I'm pretty too, too bad to mention another fella? You both think the same, that I'm pretty.

NARRATOR: Loop hops on his knees hooping himself toward her. (If it's possible lights should shine green on top of his hair)

LOOP: Little rat stop thinkin' of other men! Dogs 'ill crawl up your back if you do.

NARRATOR: He puts his hands on her hips and she falls at him laughing. They both move at each other like beach balls. Her foot catches in the jacket and he pushes at her ankle with two hands. She meanly slams her shoe into the precious leather.

LOOP: Crazy rich girl cut that out!

ANN: Hang it!

LOOP: Whut d'yu mean hang it! Have respect for a man's garment. I wear that on Sunday!

ANN: On Sunday the people laugh at you too just like on Monday. Ooooobles you're serious, so, so serious. Why'nt you kiss me? I'm a girl.

LOOP: I I I will kiss you—I would like to learn to dance, so that I can go with you to fancy places.

NARRATOR: She moves her hip closer to his and takes his hand laying it on her stomach. He grabs her mightily and they kiss.

ANN: I hear something, is it my head? There are crazy bees inside of it, you kiss crazy.

(Sounds, like those of an animal in heat, are heard.)

ANN: Listen—I hear grunts! And I think someone cussing. Don't it sound strange?

LOOP: Yus, I hear them too. Don't know why somebody should beat their animals. Terrible to do that—I would never do that.

NARRATOR: Loop and Ann move very close to where the noises come from. Futz's barn. The barn is not seen though. The noise is a human and animal one. And both people are dumbstruck at what in all heaven's holy name is happening. Something equally weird is happening to Loop; he looks insane. He pushes himself at Ann and starts to pummel her, his voice is croaky.

LOOP: Gonna rid the place of evil, gonna make you sleep a long time till your soul becomes clean.

ANN: *(She screams.)* Stop it stop it! Let me be.

NARRATOR: She tries to get away but he drags her around in a small circle.

LOOP: Gonna bury you in that evil dress, stink will in a hundred years be covered up by the sweet grass, hell isn't as bad as a whoring girl. May your father and mother not mourn you too long.

NARRATOR: Ann cries in soulful anguish. Loop drags her off. He comes back in terribly bloody clothes and sits cross-legged in the moony night. The animal sounds are louder but he shows no life, just sits with his arms folded and the hands covering his eyes. Then he slowly takes off his shoes and with a monkey's grace raises his feet to his nose and whiffs deeply.

Scene Five

NARRATOR: Cy Futz's barn again just like in the beginning. Cy is sitting with his kneebones high like the two hemispheres. The pig Amanda is sleeping on her side.

CY: Flahfy Amanda ya faymale! Four ugly legs yu got, Zeus wot hams. Luvky luck that I'm in love with you otherwise you'd be hanging in my pantry. Heeeehhhhehehehe when you're old you'll be sitting in my granny's rockin' chair readin' the Bible. Amanda you are of the world, known two kinds of male animals, pig and man! Sow I know you love me but I wonder whether you'd rather be with your own kind? Piglets I can't give you you know though I am a healthy man.

NARRATOR: Cy licks his hands passionately and praises God for making him a husbandman. Silent is his worship but the world enters his barn now. Bill Marjoram and the Sheriff Tom Sluck, slowly they go up to him. Futz yawns one eye open.

MARJORAM: There's the creep!

SLUCK: Y'all be quiet now.

MARJORAM: Quiet in hell, the biggest sinner in the world is here. If we weren't fair he'd be dead now by our own hands.

CY: I'd break them off like they were rabbits' necks.

SLUCK: Nothing is really proven yet. There will be justice.

MARJORAM: Men can make men insane!

SLUCK: Nothing is really proven yet.

MARJORAM: He drove a fella wacky!

CY: Fitz on you both boys! I know no man well enough to make him nuts. Tell me who's crazy?

SLUCK: A man's in jail now for murdering a girl, he killed because he saw something very evil.

CY: Very sad thing. But there's lotsa evil here in the world.

MARJORAM: You're the satan here in our village!

CY: I'm not anybody's keeper. I'm never near anybody. Except when they come here to see me. I just work on my little plot of land raisin' vegetables for me and my pig. What sort of evil could I have done?

NARRATOR: Cy plays a tom-tom with his feet, and salutes the sun. This is done subtly, the men not being aware of the ritual. Lord these two are blind!

SLUCK: The man who murdered an innocent girl says he did it because he was under an influence, a spell he says, because he's a simple man. Now Mr Futz I'm going to be blunt. People say here that you are an unnatural man.

CY: Am I?

SLUCK: Well, aren't you?

MARJORAM: Gods he bangs pigs!

CY: I never do. Why my mother didn't bring me up like that. I'm a Bible man.

SLUCK: If you're not serious you better become it. Very many people talk about your way.

CY: They're all wrong Mr Sluck. An animal is something to care about, not to commiteth a sin with. Soos!

MARJORAM: See what he says! Soos!

SLUCK: Soos! Soos! What does it mean?

MARJORAM: It means he be guilty and pulling our feet.

CY: Why why I never would go with an animal! I'm a village man and the sun is good on me, why I say that fellow has a devil in his head. (*He points at* MARJORAM.)

MARJORAM: Devils you bastard!

NARRATOR: He lunges at Cy and throws him down; he should not have done that though because Futz is quick and kicks his legs out cracking

Marjoram's guts hard. The Sheriff fires his pistol a warning shot into the air. Both men relax like drugged sheep.

SLUCK: There will be a trial for the man who killed the girl and he'll probably hang! The day will be Monday!

CY: I do wish they, folks, wouldn't be mean toward each other.

MARJORAM: Mean! He talks about not bein' mean! Whut about Majorie Satz? She's wretched. She's become a bigger tart than she was. She's yapping always about what he did with her and the pig with him, at the same time too he was with her. Crazy evil! Heaven help us working people with Lucifer here in our village!

SLUCK: What are you laughing for? It ain't funny when a man's going to die.

CY: I'm not killing, I'm not a judge or lawyer, just a farmer who lives poorly mindin' his own business.

MARJORAM: Well my word! You live here in the town with us. Where's your duty and responsibility?

CY: In my hands. I use them only on my land and in my barn.

SLUCK: I'm gonna tell you that I hate you myself. It isn't right that I as a lawman feel that way. The Constitution says that there should be fairness. But you ruined women, animals and a man's going to die because of you. Futz, I'm gonna do something that my sweet guts don't want, I'm gonna lock you up in the prison because the people might come here, my choppers say yes to your head under their feet, taking good revenge. But I'm gonna lock you up. You'll be safe.

CY: Who'll feed my pig and water my vegetables?

SLUCK: That's not our thought to care about your land and animals. My duty's gonna be lockin' you up in a cell.

MARJORAM: I think he needs death, not just bein' locked up. Futz had done so much harm.

SLUCK: He'll be locked up.

NARRATOR: Futz hurls up his arms as though ready to receive lightning sticks from his friend god, crash them down on the heads of his judgers who want to see him minus, with no thing, no bliss.

CY: I'm a helpless man now, a partridge run after by turkeys!

MARJORAM: Bastud. Lecherous bastud. You'll get yours for spoilin' our lives.

SLUCK: I'll be easier when you pay up your debt to us. You've done a wrong, man.

NARRATOR: Futz in the middle walks out with the men, maybe sad jazz could be played now, not too much though.

Scene Six

NARRATOR: Majorie Satz, it's another day, in the field with two men, father and brother. The first is simple. The second is complex.

FATHER: I don't know what about anything but Futz should hang though.

BROTHER NED: Like Loop, Dad. And the corpses hoss-whipped.

NARRATOR: Majorie is quiet with her arms hard against her body. She's listening like water.

FATHER: My dotter Majie is a good girl. Frisky like her reverent mother. (*He slaps* MAJORIE's *face.*)

MAJORIE: Git away from me ya old creep. Nothing was my fault!

BROTHER NED: Dad, cut it out! Nothin' is the girl's fault. She's just crazy.

FATHER: She is crazy! Should be put away!

MAJORIE: Can't be solved this way, nothing can, important thing is that I get revenged.

BROTHER NED: Nobody gonna revenge you! Nobody really cares that much.

FATHER: I care. Who's gonna marry this tramp if somehow we don't save her honor. Nobody'll git the bitch off my neck if Futz is allowed to get away with what he done. She's gotta get married off or I'll have her around our shack forever.

NARRATOR: The old man is sick by this fact of life.

FATHER: She's just got to be made respectable.

BROTHER NED: Don't Bill Marjoram want to marry her? I get the idea he'd be willing to have the ole slot machine.

MAJORIE: Shet up, ya bastud. Don't call me names.

FATHER: Control that trap! It's a wonder you haven't been killed yet being whut you are. Majorie, you're a poisonous snake. And if I didn't have to live in this village I'd kill you myself. Your daddy or not—I hate you!

NARRATOR: Does Satz mean it? I don't know.

BROTHER NED: The both of you really get me! Spoiling with fight when we got to think of something. Something where we can get Futz. I mean he should be killed! Loop is gonna be killed and Futz should also.

NARRATOR: Brother does not have much feeling when he says this. Does he have a reason for Futz's death? Yes. His sister's honor? No. Well.

FATHER: I don't want a ruckus and yet there's gotta be something to happen.

MAJORIE: What he does with animals is dirty.

BROTHER NED: HAHAHaaaahshhhhushy yeah yeah.

FATHER: Craziest thing I ever heard of.

BROTHER NED: Maybe it's good?

MAJORIE: OOOOOOOOOOOooooooooohhhh I'm sick!

FATHER: Stop your yellin', tramp. You've muddied yaself with every bloke in the village.

MAJORIE: So I have. But it's with men.

FATHER: Quit up your braggin'. Slut!

BROTHER NED: She sure is. *(He hunches over with jackal laughter.)*

Scene Seven

NARRATOR: Oscar Loop is in his cell; his mother is there. She looks like Loop, smaller of course, and wearing old things. It's the day of her boy's death.

MRS LOOP: Oscar, sweet good boy. I didn't do nothing but, but good for you I thought. I told you 'bout God when you were small and polished up your shoes for you when you went to school. I did my best for you, my son. *(She weeps.)*

LOOP: Mama, I know you did, Mama, I know you did. But let's make some plans for the wonderful things that I have. *(Takes from his pocket tiny specks of something)* Mama, these are holy bits of something good. They can cause miracles. Make people that are sick well. You know. They can even make a dead thing come alive again.

MRS LOOP: Let me hold some in my hand, maybe it'll cure my arthritis. What are they, my son?

LOOP: I call them spice-seed insects, they're alive.

NARRATOR: Mother flings her arms to the north and south, letting the insects fly. She squelches a shriek letting something dawn on her. Her son's dream.

MRS LOOP: O son, I'm sorry. But those wonderful seeds are potent, they cured my arthritis so quickly, my hands tingle.

LOOP: I knew it would work. I'm so happy. Take care of them I only have a handful. Mother use them wisely, don't give them to no pretty woman, only old people and dead things. It's a gift from Siva.

MRS LOOP: Siva? Who is Siva?

LOOP: A holy thing with lots of arms. She couldn't die with her lots of arms, even if ten brutes tried to do her in. Siva lives and lives.

MRS LOOP: Siva sounds like she's a good Christian woman. None around here like her. My son hates evil so he justly killed it. Oh son. Oh son, that you should be killed by the villagers is fair though you're my precious blood, it's right. And that you should have killed an evil girl, is right too. No! Nobody—no woman is good, all want one thing from a man, his lust stick!

LOOP: Mother mother mother *(He is weeping.)* mother mother mother why couldn't I find you? Why couldn't I ha' been my own father.

MRS LOOP: Stop it my son *(She is slightly smiling.)*, that is not a thing to say, but we two are godly and there shall be rest for us both. A son and his mother are godly.

LOOP: A son-and-his-mother-are-godly. Everything you say is beautiful. Mother, you are like the holy virgin.

MRS LOOP: That is blasphemy, son. Never say that. Look! Look! Look at me, my boy, watch me. Don't talk—just look at me. See my eyes and nose and lips? Remember my face good so that you see it on the inside of the black hood—Oooo I shouldn't say that but it's all so important to me, that when after—when you are dead they'll come to be with me and grieve. But if they don't? I couldn't stand it, I must feel them all around me, they must be a loving family all around me, they must feel so sorry for me because I am a mother with no son.

LOOP: Nothin' nothin' nothin'...

MRS LOOP: Whut?

LOOP: I'm gonna be nothin'... *(He rubs his feet on the floor.)* ...nothin'—so? Mother, who's gonna be with you? The folks you like?

MRS LOOP: Yes. But they've made my life very hard. I need them though. You wouldn't know being a man. You're my son and if you were a minister I couldn't be more proud. I'm saying everything now. I remember when you got tattooed. You said it was manly. I wasn't more proud. *(She opens her bag and lifts out a square package.)* I remember when Howard bopped me. Take some fruitcake, son. Your father was jealous of me, you wouldn't dream that I was a good-looking girl to look at me now, but I was and Howard was very jealous of me. You look like me you know, when I was young. And he would say he'd kill me too, you know, even before you were born when you was just the fruit of my womb. I'm an old woman now and have not one bit a thing. When I was young I coulda had a lot, cause of my looks. I didn't want anything, just to be happy.

LOOP: Mom—wouldn't it be wonderful if I could make myself invisible? Then I could go away. They couldn't find me. You and me would finally be let alone.

MRS LOOP: Yes, it would be wonaful *(She's almost in a trance.)* Oscar, I forgive you for wanting me to die.

LOOP: Mama, I never meant that really.

MRS LOOP: I know you didn't. I'm sorry I said that.

LOOP: You couldn't die anyway, 'cause I'd give you the spice insects.

NARRATOR: They look at each other as if he's a tot learning to walk. Noise is heard, it's time for Loop to die. When he's dead he won't see any more.

WARDEN: Hello Mrs Loop and Oscar. Mrs Loop go to my cousin Hattie, she's outside waiting to take you home with her. Oscar you come with me to the middle of town. Right?

LOOP: Right, yes yes, right. I'm bad. But I'm gonna keep my feet together when I swing like a soldier.

MRS LOOP: He's gonna look like a minister high on the pulpit above the congregation. I'm going to dress respectably.

Scene Eight

NARRATOR: Majorie in a whorey mood, walking with two drunken blokes in the field.

MAJORIE: Runnin' bastud. Futz's so scared now.

SUGFORD: Aaaa harrrr that's good.

BUFORD: Pooos. Scared yella. Uuuuuuuuuuuch my stomach hurts.

MAJORIE: You have your stomach—Cy's not gonna have his.

SUGFORD: Yeah yeah.

BUFORD: Gal that was a *creazzy* thing to do with you. I wouldn't ha' done that, I'm bagged.

SUGFORD: You bagged? I'm alive.

MAJORIE: I'm alive too.

NARRATOR: She sits on the grass, the two get down on her sides.

MAJORIE: I'm wanting excitement.

SUGFORD: Maybe you need to get banged.

BUFORD: Me too.

MAJORIE: *(Laughing high)* What for?

BUFORD: Wha'ya mean, wha'for? For fun.

NARRATOR: He picks up a stone and throws it at her. She catches it and starts playing with it, hands cupping it like its a baby chick.

MAJORIE: Let's go nuts us three then clean up somehow.

Scene Nine

NARRATOR: A little time later.

MAJORIE: Noooooot enough noooot enough!

SUGFORD: We gotta fix it good.

BUFORD: Gal, you're a pig. *(He coughs; then laughs like a madman.)*

SUGFORD: Yeah, she's a pig. We should chop her up with the other one.

MAJORIE: It's too late and I'd be dreary eating. I'm revengeful. Look I know where it is! His sow. Let's kill her. Let's kill his pig!

BUFORD: So what for? So? Fat pig wants to kill a pig.

SUGFORD: Wou'nt that be like killing yu sister?

MAJORIE: Both of you are like mice! Just wanting...

BUFORD: Git off it.

SUGFORD: Girly git off it. You're just askin' for it.

BUFORD: You don't know how you could end up.

MAJORIE: You don' have to do nothin'. I'll just do it.

SUGFORD: Why?

MAJORIE: Because I want to.

SUGFORD: Buf?

BUFORD: Okay.

Scene Ten

NARRATOR: Everything is the same.

SUGFORD: Who wants it?

MAJORIE: She's a dirty dirty thing.

SUGFORD: I'm getting away from totty. You don' want to stay here any more, do you?

BUFORD: No. Let's just gooooo.

(BUFORD *and* SUGFORD *run off.*)

MAJORIE: Come back, ya chicken bastards.

NARRATOR: Hell hath no fury like a woman scorned by a man—for a pig.

Scene Eleven

NARRATOR: In the prison cell Futz sits very hard. He's blowing out his cheeks and binding his nostrils close to the bone.

CY: Huh uuh-huh-hh-uuh- Oooooook huuhhhhoooookiioooook huuuuuh-uuuuhuh-huuuuoook ook Amaaaanddddaaaaa I mis you SOOOOOO, my molly Amaaaaandaaaaa I miiiiiiiisssss youuuuuuu. Tain't faih my faymale. You were good to me 'nd I was sooo good to you. You ate corn 'nd sleep beside me. We tried to go to church but they wouldn't let us in so I'd read you the Bible at home. My mother was a good Protistin, she'd love you too. Mother, get back in your grave you're stinkin' up the green world!

(WARDEN *comes in.*)

WARDEN: Behave yourself. Isn't there any decency in you? Dishonorin' your parents memory screaming out blasphemies in prison.

CY: Warden, you look like a bad drawing of God.

WARDEN: Futz, I should let the folks take you to them. I should hand you over to them. They'd teach your dead body manners.

CY: You want a war.

WARDEN: I want you legally killed.

CY: You don't have to fear I'll rape your mother she's too old. Or your daughter she's got your bad teeth. Warden, why don't you kill your wife and kids? You know that you're unhappy.

WARDEN: I'm a normal man, Futz. It's you that's unhappy. And you've caused treachery.

CY: I wasn't near people. They came to me and looked under my trousers all the way up to their dirty hearts. They minded my *own* life. O you're making me be so serious. And I'm only serious with my wife.

WARDEN: Your what?

CY: *(Screaming)* My wife my wife! And how many tits does your wife have? Mine has twelve.

WARDEN: You're ranting, animal.

CY: If I was wi' her I'd be grunting.

Scene Twelve

NARRATOR: It's Satz's place. Dirty. The old man, son and mother are there.

MOTHER: Majorie's such a bitch.

FATHER: It must ov been the bug's fault when she was born.

MOTHER: What d'ye mean?

FATHER: I saw a bug on your stomach when she yipped.

MOTHER: I was clean when the child was born.

FATHER: Clean as a swamp.

MOTHER: Swamp! Swamp! No. It was pure water that they had on me.

FATHER: Pig piss it was! Why, woman, you're still slying and lying!

MOTHER: I'm not gon' to say the story any more.

FATHER: Look! Look! The girl is not mine. Not my dotter.

MOTHER: She is she is she is!

FATHER: She is my dotter? Then why did the bugs sit on your knees crying prayers to heaven?

MOTHER: It didna happen!

FATHER: It could ov been you with the pig and him—like it was her!

MOTHER: I'll call my son. (Screaming) Ned! Ned!

(BROTHER NED comes in.)

FATHER: Ned Ned—be dead!

MOTHER: Hear him!

FATHER: Everythin's made her nervous, Ned. She's mad again.

BROTHER NED: Don't be mad. Majorie'll get her honor back again I'm going to kill Futz.

FATHER: Don't do it alone, take someone with you.

BROTHER NED: I want to myself.

MOTHER: (Crying) But wash with pure water, don' leave the blood.

FATHER: He could leave the blood. There's no disgrace in fightin' for his sister.

BROTHER NED: HAHuuuhahahashus hahhas hohaaahh—Mother, don't fret I won' leave the blood.

MOTHER: Before you go, will you have somethin' to eat?

Scene Thirteen

NARRATOR: He's in the prison with Cy. Ned.

CY: Boy boy boy. You want to kill me. Why?

BROTHER NED: My family.

CY: I've got none just a sow.

BROTHER NED: You make my brains red.

CY: I'll tell you peace.

BROTHER NED: (Screaming) Shut up shut up! I don't want to know you!

CY: You don't have to know me—just let me be.

BROTHER NED: (Cold fury) Your neck should be boiled.

CY: That's what I don't want to happen to my sow.

BROTHER NED: She'll die too.

CY: Now why Ned why do you want to kill the animal?

BROTHER NED: (Seething) You make my brains red! (He stabs CY.)

NARRATOR: (Ironical) Amanda—there's someone here he needs you. Yes.

(Blackout)

END OF PLAY

KONTRAPTION

KONTRAPTION was first produced on 9 February 1978 by the New York Theater Strategy at the Westbeth Theater. The cast and creative contributors were:

ABDAL . . . . Ernest Wiggins
HORTTEN . . . . .Scott Kanoff
STRAUSS . . . . Larry Fishman
GASTOUR . . . . .Julius L Webster
WIXHELI . . . . Mary Jay
CYNTHYA . . . . Yvonne Monique Lumsden
CHEMIST . . . . .Steve A Heisler
FANCHAR . . . . .Karen Elise Swanson
RONALD . . . . .Julius L Webster
PIA . . . . Yvonne Monique Lumsden
BROWD . . . . Mark Simon
EDGAHL . . . . Mark Simon
HAMFER . . . . .Julius L Webster
STARKLED . . . . Mark Simon

Director . . . . Barbara Rosoff
Set . . . . Mitchell Greenberg
Lighting . . . . .Geoffrey T Cunningham
Costumes . . . . .Bernard Roth
Masks . . . . Kevin Golden
Production stage manager . . . . Stephen Gould

CHARACTERS

ABDAL: *a black man*
HORTTEN: *a white man*
STRAUSS: *a laundryman*
GASTOUR: STRAUSS's *fantasy ideal of himself*
WIXHELI & CYNTHYA: *girls of* GASTOUR's
CHEMIST: *the powerful changer, transformer*
FANCHAR, RONALD & PIA: *fantasies of* ABDAL *and* HORTTEN
BROWD, EDGAHL, HAMFER & STARKLED: FANCHAR's *men*

AUTHOR'S NOTE

The essence of this play called KONTRAPTION goes beyond naturalism or conventional theatre logic. The roots of the play are wound up with cultural ideals, myths, and sensibilities. The truths fracture into facets of human longing and experience. It is essential that the director keep in mind the transformations of rhythm, images, and sound values within the language. The actor has worlds within worlds to play. All the elements of humor must be achieved so that the darker aspects will emerge with greater impact.

(ABDAL *and* HORTTEN *are friends and they experience, create, and transform the realities of their lives. Here they are on an empty terrain. Where might they be next? There is a water tower nearby.* ABDAL *holds his hands over his friend's face.*)

HORTTEN: You're preventing the air from going into my nose!

(ABDAL *stares blankly, removes his hands.*)

ABDAL: I know. Oh, I was only playing with you. I'd never block up your passages. Your ole orifices. Your ole nose holes. Your openings. You are my...duck. My lil fat white duck, whose feathers should be oily and fine, soft, very soft. I should rub you all over with coconut oil or heart...of palm oil...or oil...of rose...water...and then I'd take a match and burn your buttocks off!

HORTTEN: What a sick thing to say! You know you break my heart into bits when you say things like that!

ABDAL: It's rare when I say that kinda thing. It's just so bad the way things are...between us...our friendship.

HORTTEN: No! We have fun! We have fun together! (*He sees a roach and crushes it.*)

ABDAL: Aren't you going to wash your hand after touching the roach?

HORTTEN: I don't have to because I'm not going to touch my mouth or my eyes.

ABDAL: Well, don't touch me unless you wash.

HORTTEN: Don't worry, Abdal. Abdal, let's read from *Tristan und Iseult*.

ABDAL: No. It's too late.

HORTTEN: Oh, just a bit of *Tristan und Iseult*.

ABDAL: No reading from that fuckin' book!

HORTTEN: This anger is not good for me!

ABDAL: I'm mad too!

HORTTEN: Tristan will fix that. Trust me, Abdal. (*He reads from book.*) "For he trusted in God and knew no man dared to draw sword against him and truly he did well to trust in God, for though the felons mocked him when he said he loved loyally, yet I call you to witness My Lords who read this and who know of the philter drunk upon the high seas, and who understood whether his love were disloyalty indeed. Forever see this and that outward thing, but God alone, the heart, and in the heart alone is crime and the sole final judge is God."

ABDAL: *(Smiling)* And in the heart alone is crime.

(A buzzer rings. ABDAL goes offstage. We hear his voice and the voice of the laundryman, MR STRAUSS.)

ABDAL'S VOICE: Oh, I'm....*(Laugh)* Nice day. *(Laugh)* You're early. *(Laugh)* You have had coffee? Oh the sunshine! *(Laugh)*

STRAUSS'S VOICE: I deliver du shtuff, mine stomach pliss! Oooooof! Full last nicht. *(Coughs)* Heavy doughnuts like baby's cheeks! Oooo gee vah! Bik folds on mine behind, so sore mine rectum te-tum.

ABDAL'S VOICE: Well, do come in. Oh, Hortten, Mr Strauss is here to pick up our laundry. Get the bag, Hortten!

(STRAUSS and ABDAL appear. STRAUSS touches his backside constantly, testing his own existence. HORTTEN drags a huge cloth bag in.)

STRAUSS: I don't never wish I betchya do it should happen to you, it should feel like such a terrible inchury in the skin like a child's red mouth OOOO! It hurts me! Pliss!

HORTTEN: He's going to ask! He's going to ask us, Abdal, now!

STRAUSS: *(Frantic)* Pliss let me sit down and rest here!

ABDAL: Nooo! What does he think this is, Hortten? A public resting place! This ain't no public toilet!

STRAUSS: But I have to, pliss! Pliss! Mine suppers! Vot's old! Pliss, fah God's self-love! His gootness! Your kindness! Such good nice men! Your charity! Now und then I ask you, a human being, an urge, I'm human, don't feel mean, it's a natural order. I loosen my fingers, my heart at you, hav a heart, mine Gott! I sing with a tiny little bird's tongue, ve all draw in varm air, life! Ve all breathe! Yiy yiy! It's so thick und it's cushiony, a cargo of roses!

ABDAL: No! No! I'll pick your goddamn flesh off first! Slob! Slob! No! Slob! Slob! Pig! Slob!

STRAUSS: *(Waving hands gracefully, telling a story)* Und out of a window I see elm trees und clouds so vhite und yella duffadills und rododendrums, tossing horses und cows mit bik juicy eyes, a mama holting mine hand, a papa giffing me a shiny penny, a loving tante kissing a bread crumb avay from a baby's cheeks. *(To ABDAL.)* You! You vant to poot dirt on mine face! On my heart! You vant to put dirt! But I'll grab! I'll hold! I'll holt on to you!

(STRAUSS lunges at ABDAL. HORTTEN faces the audience, closes his eyes and sticks his fingers into his ears.)

ABDAL: Strauss! You don't look or smell good! You smell like rotten meat!

STRAUSS: Vy shoult a man smell like a voman's perfumed elbows, vy? Und ven I was young und I vas a tree! An oak tree I vas mit enerchetic moofments!

(A muscular man rolls across; two chattering females joyfully watch and admire him. STRAUSS has conjured them all up. ABDAL and HORTTEN are stunned.)

GASTOUR: *(To the females)* My wrists are tougher than—

WIXHELI: Iron pipes!

CYNTHYA: Iron pots!

GASTOUR: Scums, slippery, slippery, drip and sweat, O all pulse, plump bunched roots! *(His voice is rhythmic, poetic.)* Who wants a third thump? Who wants to be turned? Who wants a sleek otter without a wrinkle in it? Who wants to be nibbled during a calm morning? Stay all night! Caress, touch the muscles of my lips. *(Yawns)* Sleepy, sleepy, but first hungry hungry!

(He scoops invisible food out of the bellies of the females. They scoop food out of each other.)

GASTOUR: Do not separate the bones but pick meat off very carefully! And leave all sinews attached on this earth. Try to be careful! You give me hard tasks, girls! I must watch my scalp with you! If I were in a boat on the sea—you two would gnaw holes in my boat!

ABDAL: Who are you! Who are you!

GASTOUR: I am chief! The women watch the fields and adorn me! And place my headdress on my head. And they need fear nothing! And I have a good-looking woman to lie with when I want one or maybe both at one time! I dip my cock into one and then into the other. No one envies anybody. It is good!

STRAUSS: They luf you! They luf you!

GASTOUR: I have been created big! I tramp the earth down deep! I throw birds farther up into the sky!

STRAUSS: I am fearless! Yiy yiy you are fearless!

GASTOUR: When I decide that something should die—I plunge it into a hole with fat! I make the women jump into water to get berries, fruit!

ABDAL: What are the females called!

GASTOUR: Scratch-Rump! I call them Scratch-Rump! One is never without the other. And when I'm with both of them, I'm more than a man—I'm a buffalo! I have strength to hump the world! I eat the heart of a whale and its gizzard! Who here has eaten whale heart! Or whale gizzard! It's big and dirty! ·

(Females giggle.)

GASTOUR: You like that! Big and dirty gizzard! Big and dirty gizzard!
Hot whale heart! I'll fuck you up to your eyes!

(They laugh and disappear.)

STRAUSS: I used to moof like a billy goat! So light on my feet I vas! So goot
I vould felt—so young! So strong! I vas a billy goat! So full of powerful
feelinks! Please! I vould like to sit down!

*(ABDAL takes a plastic bag, goes behind STRAUSS and puts it over his head.
HORTTEN faces audience and sticks his fingers into his ears as the gasping sounds
of STRAUSS are heard. He dies. ABDAL stretches and does neck exercises beside the
body.)*

ABDAL: *(Reciting)* "I asked a thief to steal me a peach, he turns up his eyes I
asked a lithe lady to lie her down holy and meek she cries, as soon as I went
an angel came, he winked at the thief and smiled at the dame and without
one word spoke had a peach from the tree and twixt earnest and joke
enjoyed the lady."

(HORTTEN goes to ABDAL.)

HORTTEN: Hortten!...I'm Hortten! Abdal! You're Abdal! Abdal, which is
more, the land or the sea? Abdal, which came first, the day or the night?

ABDAL: Which came first the day or the night! Goddamn you, you
mother—and your riddle games! The night came first! The night!
Corn shoots out of the ground in the night! In the dark!

HORTTEN: Abdal, why did you kill Strauss?

ABDAL: Another riddle game, little white duck? All-wise Hortten in the
clear light of day. I won't say why I killed Strauss.

HORTTEN: You killed him because he wanted to sit down and rest here.

ABDAL: Maybe yes, maybe no. Dostobas geraten rolle. Ach!
Ach! German's a goot lank...vitch! Ja wohl!

HORTTEN: Did you kill Mr Strauss because he was German? He wasn't,
Abdal, you know he wasn't. He wasn't a real German. He was an Albanian!
Originally he was an Albanian. Albania's far from Germany. He had an
Albanian name! His name was Edrushlucos. And he merely changed it to
Strauss.

ABDAL: Merely! Hard shit! Merely! My nose! Merely! Up your neck pipe!
Merely! Hoo hah! No, I didn't kill him because he was a German and I don't
give a simple ass damn or a stiff tit about him being an Albanian or a
mother! *(Weepy)* I'll die of grief one day! Get off from the backs of my heels!
Stop nailing down my heels! You're never going to know why I killed
Strauss! You twin mother!

HORTTEN: I'm a solitary, Abdal. Not a twin!

ABDAL: You're a twin to a lump of rotting blutwurst! Strauss is dead because he wanted!! *(Melodramatic)* I did not pity Strauss through human identification with him... with my love longings. I blocked my ears and eyes, stuffed them up like you. And I shuddered along with him, Strauss the laundryman! Me, a black man who works in a delicatessen. Hoo! Hah! The storm took us both! His dying body shuddered and I shuddered with a tragic emotion! Pity and terror! Hoo! Hah! I could have killed him twenty more times!

HORTTEN: Lives had, I mean, have been spoiled by love and by bad luck! I'll pray for you for your peace!

ABDAL: I'll pray for your ass! You know you are blind!

HORTTEN: You mean that I don't know the events in this world. Do you mean that?

ABDAL: *(Dancing)*
Whenever you want me, I'll
Be there, I'll be right there.
You can want,
You can need,
You can want me
Whenever you want me.

HORTTEN: Abdal, this is a much troubled time and place. We dig ourselves deliberately into the darkness. We should touch each other!

ABDAL: Yes, mmmhuh! Put our fingers into each other's hearts!

HORTTEN: Abdal, we all hide our sins from each other. I won't reveal the secret coloring of my sin! My own sin! *(Feigns weeping)*

ABDAL: Is it ugly? Is it real, you simple ass!

HORTTEN: I love artifice! It's the love of artifice! Yes, I love artifice!

ABDAL: That ain't nothin' new—you love fakery! You love fakery and not a line of truth!

HORTTEN: Is it the course of my nature? Is that the course of my nature? Can it destroy me?

ABDAL: *(Smiling)* No, it won't...rend you.

HORTTEN: You mean I won't die? Abdal, I won't die?

ABDAL: No. You'll be bewildered, Hortten. Just bewildered.

HORTTEN: "What merit or what favor showeth thee to me?"

(Time passes.)

(ABDAL, *looking at a mirror, pats his bald head and smells his fingers.*)

ABDAL: Just a bald man. An agreeable bald man. Myrrh and sweet herbs, my head smells fragrantly of myrrh and sweet herbs. No gloom on my brow, no corruption, no weakness, no tedium.... And I fear nothing! Nothing can be stolen from me. Not my sharp mind, and especially not my sweet odors. What a pleasure and what a virtue in me being me! I am not an actor, nor a mime. I act my own role! Simply, like a beast, like a good beast, an obedient animal. I persevere under His rule and keep His commandments! O Lord! My legs, my legs! I put them apart. I stand in the garden of delight. Peace passes all understanding. (*Pause, tense*) How much more wonderful when the world was young and wild! (*He bites his wrist, drawing blood.*) Lazarus, come forth! A man four days dead stinks! My free will causes righteousness...or transgression! A child of love and death! O Lord! In my own eyes I am a monk but my garments are...my garments... my garments are impure. (*He winks and grins.*) I am one of the dregs under heaven, all tangled up like a bundle, a bundle, tangled up with a yoke of bondage. I lick my lips and cry out: A fool is Christ! I want to lay him! And I will lay treasures up on earth and not in heaven! I am a mourner. I am one of the meek, one of the hungry, a persecuted one, a reviled one, one of the poor in spirit, the spiritless poor. One of them that he blessed in the Sermon on the Mount. Though I be free from all men, yet have I made myself servant unto all, that I might gain the more. My sweat is sweet. My sweat is a sweet sauce. I shall dip bread and olives into my own liquid, my juice! How useless, how vain to sing out water, water, water when I can drink myself! When ye can drink up the green herb's juice! When ye can eat... the green lizard half raw!

(HORTTEN *appears.*)

HORTTEN: Here is the fat—here am I! White duck! Here is the fat white duck! Duck white fat!

ABDAL: (*Angry*) Suck metal! Suck cold, ugly metal! Hortten, you're wrong! You're spoiling it! My time! My role! You're full of shit! Faultfinder! Have you ever known a woman with concave nipples...that a kiss could, could... (*He stuffs fingers into mouth.*)

HORTTEN: Abdal, Strauss was a man, his goodness was good, et cetera, etcetera. He had he had he had he had he had he had he had he had he had had haddddhaddd heard his own groans of pain! He had he had he had he had hadddd when he died! Albanian, German, a man's a man for a' that! All of us were, are, one man! One man we are! Were! Chains of death forcing us down! Indecently our nakedness peeks through the fig leaves! Our fingers cramp as we try to hold the leaves together. The heavy chunk is stiff-necked and rips through the leaves! Abdal, you made crime! You killed an Albanian and a German! Two races! Abdal, I accuse you of being a racist! Of feeling no pity for human frailty, etcetera. Sex, natural conditions, natural conditions, conditions, conditions, Abdal! Can! Can, can, can can, cannnnn choke a man to death!

ABDAL: *(Singing)* What are you doing to the people,
I have come upon you, caught you
Doing something to the people,
And all the heads are flesh-drained.

(The CHEMIST appears. He is powerful and unearthly.)

CHEMIST: *(To ABDAL)* I smelt your fear.

ABDAL: *(Singing)* A question sits on top of my neck,
It flops like a satin ribbon,
A man's head,
And I sit laughing out my
Million injuries.
I skim my happy lids
Over my vicious eyeballs,
My mouth lengthens
With happiness. O people,
O my children,
My children's bones!

CHEMIST: The trouble is not your bones! Your bones, no, are not calcium poor! No, they are rich! Very rich! Your assbone is sharp as a knife! *(Laughs)* You can dig your own assbone into a tender cheek. *(Intense)* The bird laughs at the worm because he is wrongly made! Put together very ugly! The bird is his own God! He only is natural! *(To audience)* Who is wrongly made? Who is put together? Very ugly? Who is his own? God? Who only is natural? Who are the worms? Not you, me, you?

ABDAL: At night I try to eat myself, my neck, my neck is too short! I am hard and vengeful, hard and vengeful! My eyes, my lips, my ankles, my feet! God, that I would be whole again!

CHEMIST: *(Going to ABDAL and holding a knife to his throat)* The mountain is a female, calm and fair! Lie down, you!

ABDAL: This is a nightmare! This is a nightmare! Your breath in my ear is a nightmare! Don't kill me! Don't leap on top of me! Don't dig your evil kneebones into my face! Insect! Insect! Don't kill me! Don't open me! Don't open me!

CHEMIST: *(Knocking ABDAL out)* He will grow younger and he will tell funny stories and he will go among the people and smell out their fears, their evil. And Abdal will think about women's knees and veins, pain. The glitter of silver fillings in their teeth. *(He constructs a new body for ABDAL. He creates a high and broad shape, an absurd squarish form that begins out of ABDAL's under-arms.)* Why had I found Abdal? Come to him? Saw Abdal? I smelled his fear, his longing! His longing is food for the soul!

HORTTEN: *(Terrified)* Do not eat Abdal! He is not food!

CHEMIST: Pig! Dog! There are laws proper to each being!
Between matter and spirit there is harmony! Spirit and body, fire and water, soft and hard. There is harmony!

HORTTEN: I thought that you were going to eat Abdal. I thought only that you were going to eat him! I meant no harm!

CHEMIST: I am the maker! The maker of shapes and forms! He is of two natures. The animal and the mechanical!
A marvelous fact of nature. Abdal holds a special place in the universe!
A new breed of man! Not humdrum! But he, Abdal, shall partake in the new heaven and earth! Intelligence and technology lay nature open to plain view! Art and nature! Art and nature! With my skill, my tool! My tool! I humanize the world! I humanize it! I am part of a voluptuous contest!

HORTTEN: Voluptuous contest?

CHEMIST: Science and mystery fight and complement each other! The exaltation of nature! Look at this religious soul, Abdal! This tender and sensual false-ass. Abdal, wake up! Stand up! You are a new man today. Your judgment is much sharper now! I blush with pity at how you were made before I happened along to transform your external shape. Now you are a perfect man! There is more soul in your face now. Abdal, turn your face to me. Ah, you are a blending of nature and graceful art! A perfect man of a solid and lasting civilization! *(To audience.)* Ah, listening? Ah, seeing? Ah, fake-ass? You there! Ours alone? False-ass, look sharp! Are you listening? A man flaunts his rebirth! His new beginning! I mean no harm! I have my ideals! My impulses also. What does one need a great and bloody body for? It will just only, once only, detach itself from life and rot!

(ABDAL begins to walk.)

CHEMIST: Look at this prince! Look at him swagger! Look at him praise life like beating drums praise the rain! I think I want to weep! I feel so jolly! I've tapped the sap of perfection! When the natural part, the vulnerable segment, the bloody meat portion goes, hips and ass go on!

HORTTEN: Hips and ass go on?

CHEMIST: Yes, hips and ass go on!

HORTTEN: Without the rest?

CHEMIST: Who needs that which will die!

HORTTEN: But the flesh is sublime!

CHEMIST: Sublime. What a false word! What a false word to describe the flesh! Hips and ass go on!

HORTTEN: Wandering about by themselves? Hips and ass? Alone, all alone?

CHEMIST: I have seen eyes float alone without a face surrounding them! And lips!

HORTTEN: Lips?

CHEMIST: Lips! And always puckered for a kiss!

HORTTEN: Can Abdal function? Can Abdal function correctly?

CHEMIST: Of course! Would I do less than nature! Abdal can fart like a beast! Like a horse!

HORTTEN: All is not lost then. The part of Abdal closest to the worst—no, Abdal's worst part—lives forever! It cannot be killed!

CHEMIST: Like Mr Strauss was killed. No, no—hips and ass go on! Like triumphant soldiers home from holy wars! Like a thousand butterflies released from a thousand cocoons! On and on they go on! Hips and ass go on! Hips and ass go on! Hips and ass go on! High up in the mountains and low down in the valleys, choruses will chime: Hips and ass go on! Hips and ass go on! It will become a tradition old as the Greeks' and Hebrews'! A maxim will be: Which came first, hips or ass!

HORTTEN: You are so funny!

CHEMIST: Like a plunging abyss. Think where water comes from. Think what is dead.

(ABDAL *dances.*)

CHEMIST: See, Abdal is playing!

HORTTEN: Abdal, what are you playing?

CHEMIST: He won't talk for a while. His tongue is shocked! I'll tell you what Abdal is playing. He is playing a dance! Abdal is dancing!

(ABDAL's *dance changes to a military challenge. His movements alter to anguish and violence. He slowly changes his mood to joy and sits.*)

CHEMIST: Don't you want to vomit with his bliss?

ABDAL: *(Singing)* Hips and ass go to and fro
On this good good earth.
I want to see the sacred game
That fed my body's girth,
That fed my body's birth!

CHEMIST: Original! Like science, law, and war!

HORTTEN: How happy Abdal is! He moves me! Abdal moves me! One night we were in the woods, lying down with our fingers touching! How human it was!

CHEMIST: Indeed, indeed how human. Did you notice it is cold now? I think we should make a tent. We have canvas—

HORTTEN: But we have no frame for the canvas. What about a frame?

CHEMIST: Abdal is square and sturdy. His frame is square and sturdy.

HORTTEN: Square and sturdy?

CHEMIST: Abdal will be our tent and protect us from the cold! (CHEMIST *leaves.*)

HORTTEN: Abdal, I am your friend and...

(HORTTEN *hands him some bread.* ABDAL *eats the bread. The mood is peaceful.*)

HORTTEN: Robbery outside, tyranny outside, war outside, men biting! Women biting! Breathing, snorting, death croakings outside! But you take the bread that I give you. You reach out with four fingers and take the bread that I give—with my fingers...you take the bread that I give you—it's good, dark bread. I want us to eat good bread—you take the bread with the fingers that have touched me...

ABDAL: *(Gentle)* I love your bread...you care what kind of bread I eat or if I have bread to eat. You are my...my friend. Where is cheese?

HORTTEN: Where is Strauss?

ABDAL: Where is cheese?

HORTTEN: Strauss, Strauss.

ABDAL: Cheese, I said cheese...don't...don't....O just forget about...cheese. Strauss is in my mouth, you detective! He's in with the cheese.

HORTTEN: But you have only bread in your mouth—no cheese!

ABDAL: And no Strauss! No Strauss! No Strauss! You gawdamn louse! No Strauss, no Strauss, or Mrs Strauss! No Strauss! Forget him. His memory—his aftertaste!

HORTTEN: In my nose! I can taste Strauss in my nose!

ABDAL: You are nauseating me! Listen, Strauss's holiness is not lost! His aether lives!

HORTTEN: That's good...I...that's good...I feel better. *(He stares at* ABDAL's *body.)*

ABDAL: What's wrong? What is wrong? What is wrong!

HORTTEN: Hips and ass! The song....the song!

ABDAL: *(Singing)* Hips and ass go to and fro
On this good good earth.
I want to see the sacred game
That fed my body's birth.

(CHEMIST appears.)

CHEMIST: It's cold. It's cold. I think we should make a tent. Abdal is square and sturdy. His frame is square and sturdy! Abdal will be our tent and protect us from the cold. *(He hangs cloth over ABDAL.)*

ABDAL: *(Singing)* Hips and ass go to and fro
On this good good earth.
I want to see the sacred game
That fed my body's birth.
Hips and ass go to and fro
On this good good earth.
I want to see the sacred game
That fed my body's girth!

(Prayer: Dangling Savior Incantation)

ABDAL: Cruel, cannibalistic! Sweet Jesus! Dangling savior protect us from cold or I'll chew you up for treason! Preach the word, I'll do it! I'll do it I'll do it I can't stand no one here can stand the violence! Give us something gentle! Not cruel! Human, human, human, make us be gentle, human, human, make us not ferocious, make us quit the leer! Dangling savior O! O strong in work and war, O huge love, O wet space, O wet cruel cruel savior of juice, O emerald! Veined phallus! O pure crystal sperm, wringing love ferocious, hound maw, O Christ muzzle, O gold mucus, O dark blue, O dark blue, O savage, savage pips and pits ass and hips, good, good earth! You will live for kingdom is up high, high! Child of sneers! Put the rubber gloves on! Pork-roast God! Swine mother! Give us kindliness for punishment! Fat sausage give us a diamond pecker to screw eternally like the dogs and locusts! O eater! O Mater! O Mater with grandmothers and old men! O bull-calf lover! O worshiper of nipples and long teeth! O sweet giblet! Sinning faithless Christian! Roman! Goth! African! Banana! Cucumber! Horse-leg! Finger of indecency! Banging eyelid! Eyelid of Satan! Of Columbus! Of Pius XII! Of monkey! Of liars! Of poisoned wells! Plague! America! Money eater! Silk stuffer! Quencher! Chomper! Mugger! Slayer! Boaster! Panther! Blood fist! Death vegetable! Flock humper! Tree! Tree! Tree! O rag! O bloody god of bandages! Of bottle tops! Of sweating yellow cafeterias! Carnal fire hose! Frozen torture! Gentle! Gentle! Supply us! Supply us with good! Delight us with good! I am the meat! Ich bin das Fleisch! Yah! Yah! Gootertank! Fleisch! Fleisch! Fleisch! Owfowfowf! Owfveedayrzayn! Strauss! Strauss! Strauss! Ich bin ein Berliner! Hey Joe, vere's de sowsage! I am the meat that dances, American-style! Ich bin ein American Fleisch! I am a musical asshole! Kinder! Kinder! Bread! Austria?

Germany? America? Professor Strauss speaks English! The best buy I ever saw in Europe is meat! Hot and cold meat! Clean! Fleisch! You got spotless meat! Pfennigs! Drachmas! Pennys! Nipples! Meat buttons! I see amazing things! Prices start at twenty shillings! Drachmas! Mezuzahs! Thirty nipples buy you adequate meat! The owners of meat are hospitable and speak German, Albanian, French, and Colorado Springs! The starvation has a wealth of its own! The meat is so dignified!

(HORTTEN *and* CHEMIST *arrange different tent shapes on* ABDAL. *As* ABDAL *becomes an Arab tent, Arabic music plays. As he becomes a Central Asian tent, Turkish music plays. American Indian tent, we hear American Indian drums. When he becomes a military tent, we hear marching-band music.* ABDAL's *face contorts and he screams.*)

ABDAL: With the assbone of a Jew!

(*A meat hook is hung by the Chemist.* ABDAL *imitates the sound of buzzing flies.* CHEMIST *and* HORTTEN *mime a hunt with wild animals.* ABDAL *becomes calm.*)

ABDAL: I could not love you dear so much loved I I I could not love you dear baby so much loved I not bot not sot. (*Garbles words over and over*)

HORTTEN: Abdal, look at me! Friend! How wonderful you are! How versatile! Abdal, Abdal, hips and assss! Hips and assss! How varied you are! Versatile! Versatile! Friend, I love you!

ABDAL: (*Defiantly*) I love myself! I could kick myself off a high cliff and leap down like a great hero and save myself! I would hold myself to myself like a child holds a bird! As tender as a kitten with its heart cut out! Or a deer mourning for another deer! Or an elephant eaten by vultures! These are tender things! And if I croaked I would mourn for myself! I would swallow up all the grief stuffed in holes. Little animals that never stood up on their legs. I would take the grief into myself and finally be satisfied like a killer whale. Like a man stealing from another man! Like a bladder being rid of hot stones!

HORTTEN: Shut up, grease box!

ABDAL: You say to me: Shut up, grease box! What!

HORTTEN: Please, shut up for—

ABDAL: For what! You nostril!

HORTTEN: Square ass!

ABDAL: Nostril! Nostril!

HORTTEN: Square ass! Square ass!

ABDAL: I'll put a sharp stick up your nose!

HORTTEN: (*Laughing*) Grease box! Grease box! Grease box!

ABDAL: Skunk! Traitor!

HORTTEN: Jew! Jew! Assbone Jew!

ABDAL: Fuck nose! Fuck nose!

HORTTEN: Snake hole! Snake hole!

ABDAL: Skin of a dead rat!

HORTTEN: Assbone! Assbone!

ABDAL: Fish nose!

HORTTEN: Fat ass! Fat ass!

ABDAL: Fish eater! Fish eater! Dirty Christian! Piece of fish!

HORTTEN: Fat ass!

ABDAL: *(Lurching at* HORTTEN*)* I'll ram you! I'll ram you!

HORTTEN: Get away or I'll pull off your balls!

ABDAL: Fish-bladder eater!

HORTTEN: Chicken shit! *(Pause. Friendly tone.)* Tide rise! Glowy moon!

ABDAL: *(Friendly)* Sweet gum of a tree!

HORTTEN: My own lovely mucus!

ABDAL: Angel gizzard!

HORTTEN: Salmon balls!

ABDAL: Groundhog baby!

HORTTEN: Human! Human!

ABDAL: *(Hugging* HORTTEN*)* Ah, friend! Friend!

HORTTEN: Friend, friend—I could drink grease for you!

ABDAL: I'd become your eternally obedient master!

HORTTEN: I'd give you the sea!

ABDAL: I'd pick you a million golden flowers!

HORTTEN: I'll steal the west wind for you!

ABDAL: I'd feed you tender gizzard every day of your life!

HORTTEN: I'll be a loving man—like Strauss! Strauss!

ABDAL: Strauss! Strauss! Y'gawdamn louse! Strauss! Strauss! Y'gawdamn louse! *(Pause)* Oh, Hortten, friend—let's obtain strength! Strength for each other! Let's slowly and surely reach out to each other and save ourselves! Let's put things back!

HORTTEN: I love your wants! Your yearnings! Your yearnings!

ABDAL: I've been a split bleeding animal for so long! *(Looks at his body)* The strangeness! Why? What's it about?

HORTTEN: You killed Strauss! And you were cursed! But it's better, a lot better, that shape, than having your head cut off! And stuffed in a tree trunk! Big hips! Big hips! Big ass! And you'll go on forever! Be glad that you're not a stick!

ABDAL: But I'm human—and this shape...this form....

HORTTEN: You killed Strauss—you killed Strauss because of his foreignness! And now you're paying the price!

(ABDAL starts to roll a cigarette. HORTTEN watches him, fascinated.)

HORTTEN: How good! How good you roll a cigarette! Can you do it with one hand? Could you roll a cigarette with one hand? That would be a whole army marching over a land if you could roll a cigarette with one hand! *(Laughs)*

ABDAL: *(Philosophizing)* Under oak and earth passion names itself! Child, cow, corn—I am moved by fogggg, mockery of myselfffff, insight into belieffffff of a past cosmological scream! I roll a cigarette well! I can be admired for it! You can see a bit of savageness in my act of rolling a cigarette. No Christian movement in my rolling...rolling a cigarette!

HORTTEN: Did Strauss smoke?

ABDAL: Excellently! Strauss smoked excellently! Good Indian tobacco! No! No! Algerian tobacco! Ahh, Strauss! *(He weeps and then the sounds change to a sad Levantine chant.)*

HORTTEN: Strauss! You weep for Strauss?

ABDAL: No, no, for my ugliness. My ugliness. O ugliness, thy desolate the the thy thy—

HORTTEN: *(To audience)* Whyfor does Abdal speak of his ugliness? Whyfor does the carrot eat up the rabbit? Tragedy! Be a magician and figure that out! Play with tits! Smoke a fag! Knock a sack of beans on the chin! Say no a first time! A second! No! The third! No! *(Screaming wildly.)* No! No! *(Pause. To ABDAL.)* You are an American!

ABDAL: No, I'm an Indian! Comanchee! And I want a woman! Beauty!

(Time passes. Four attractive and well-built men are talking to a lovely lady. We do not hear them. There is a feeling of calm, poetic beauty. After a while we hear them.)

FANCHAR: *(Gracefully using her hands)* My nature and age, what slender grounds they stand on. Loftier work is at hand.

EDGAHL: It makes me go farther on...I would like to be...be famous! You, Fanchar, carry me up with your smile.

FANCHAR: We should regard ourselves as noble people of a certain class, part of a family with parents of a name that we deserve. We drink from the spring of nobility!

BROWD: I don't want anything frivolous!

FANCHAR: You are too serious! Crave light—and joking!

HAMFER: *(Laughing)* That can be sufficient for a lifetime! Ah, Fanchar, you can make wild desire seem reasonable! And envy!

FANCHAR: *(Grandly)* With real men envy is never aroused!

STARKLED: Thank God!

BROWD: But you arouse our desire! We protect you! Ah, Fanchar, you give order, beauty to the great world!

STARKLED: Your mild lovely woman's eyes! Soft chin! Soft throat and slender fingers! Your light perfect pink nipples...I would love—

FANCHAR: A time for love! Ah, we know how very wonderful that time is! Ah, and it's so easy for us to love!

(ABDAL and HORTTEN *are watching this exquisite and lyrical fantasy of their hearts' desire.*)

STARKLED: I can't wait until I see and kiss my own sweet beautiful girl!

EDGAHL: Loving a woman and having meaningful work is terribly terribly good!

FANCHAR: Yes! This world is clamorous! Ah, so loud and very cruel! A moment can be full of evil!

EDGAHL: I notice—

FANCHAR: Yes, what do you notice?

EDGAHL: I notice how very elegant and kind your hands look. Put them on my body!

(FANCHAR *places her hand on his arm.*)

EDGAHL: See how tender and feminine they look on my body! Light pale pigeons, the tips of your fingers are pink pale bills! I must not say this, but—

BROWD: *(Angry)* Stop it, Edgahl! Fanchar is very good to be with us for this evening! Let's not dispose of our inhibitions! This is not Italy! Nor even Havana before—

FANCHAR: Before the revolution! *(Laughs)*

EDGAHL: *(Excitedly handing her a note)* Fanchar, here is a poem I've written for you! Two days ago! I should give the poem privately to you, not in front of the others!

(FANCHAR *reads the poem and, with dignity, tears it up.*)

EDGAHL: Why did you tear my poem up! Why! I love you and you tear my poem up! My poem! My heart!

FANCHAR: The poem was a bad poem! And you should not be so outraged! You assaulted me in your dreams! So I tore up the poem! You had a Coke bottle between my legs! My mouth puckered and wet!

EDGAHL: But you tore my heart up! My poem! My poem! My poem!

FANCHAR: I had to! You had not the right to use me without my wanting to be used! *(Pause)* I gave you some pfennigs two days ago and you never gave them back to me! There is a lump of evil in you!

EDGAHL: I love you! I love you!

BROWD: Ah, Edgahl, let Fanchar alone! She need not love us all the same! She might have a preference if she wants to! Let it be wonderfully enough that she is amongst us!

(BROWD *kisses her hand and* FANCHAR *kisses him on the mouth.*)

BROWD: Fanchar's kiss is warm and good. It makes me forget that the world is bad—and that there are not only Christians who live in it! *(Laughs effeminately)*

(*They all reach toward each other, then the image fades away.*)

HORTTEN: *(To* ABDAL*)* Who was the woman? A knight's lady? Ah, so pretty! Pretty! Pretty!

ABDAL: I wonder if she was under all of them!

HORTTEN: *(Angry)* They might just have been wonderful friends!

ABDAL: No! She was under them! *(He makes an obscene gesture.)* Ah, her bones, her leg bones are so fine!

HORTTEN: She is my ideal of womanliness! And civilization! And culture! And the splendid healthy men! Not one was a cripple!

ABDAL: I am not that! What! I am not that! Oh, you must mean—you're talking about someone else! Not me. I am all right! Right! All right! Hips and ass! Hips and ass go to and fro on this good, good earth, I want to see the sacred game that— *(He looks at his shape.)* Hortten, this is not the body of a crippled man! But of a gentle man. A man can be gentle! A man can be tender! Tenderness does not mean soft!

HORTTEN: Quiet! Quiet! There is nothing wrong with you or the universe! I want to mull on the image of the woman and the men. Did you notice her thighs and knees, so strong and so finely molded! I wanted to put my hands on the knees of that woman...and move them slowly...so slowly apart. Which one of the big fellows do you think, Abdal, would grab me by the neck! And force my head beneath his shoe! And smash my chest! And stick his thumbs in my eyes! Kick my ass! Smash my balls! Because of me slowly, so slowly moving the woman's knees apart! Those great strong men would protect the woman...from ugliness, danger, stinkbombs, holocaust, Yugoslavs, Japs...unwashed feet. The grace of a chivalrous age! I want to howl with joy!... Suppose the woman one day was in a fit of grief for someone. Ah, the grief of woman moves me! The sorrow of a woman, the pain of a woman, the torture of women puts tension into my fists, my mouth becomes like old wood. A piercing, I feel a piercing, an insect's sharp leg in the back of my throat. My heart becomes a bloody pillow—all my organs wail and cry out when I think about woman's sorrow...her eternal—

ABDAL: Gloomy fool! Songster! Songster! Rhymester! Cheap poet! Tin Pan Alley! Valentine slop! Third-rate priest! Gonif! Gonif! Bullshit! Liar!

HORTTEN: It's not a lie! I am attuned to woman, man, and child!

ABDAL: The hipbone's connected to the assbone! Your balls and ass!

HORTTEN: So you do not believe that in me is great sympathy!

ABDAL: Sympathy! Shmimpathy! You'd piss on a baby cat!

HORTTEN: I would not!

ABDAL: You'd kill and roast your best friend! You'd give feces to a starving man!

HORTTEN: Why—why don't you trust me?

ABDAL: Because you are a fat, guilty fellow and a smell comes from you!

HORTTEN: A smell from me!

ABDAL: Yes, you smell like a pig!

HORTTEN: Pshaw! Pshaw! Pshaw!

ABDAL: You are a stinking stinking, guilty fellow!

HORTTEN: *(Placating)* Let's eat some food! Let's eat now. We're hungry!

ABDAL: I'm too angry to eat!

HORTTEN: Let's run a race then! It'll burn the anger up! Let's run a race and let the one who wins...be the chief!

ABDAL: Chief of what?

HORTTEN: It's just a game. The one who loses will dish out the food. The pot with the food is to be the goal—and the one who touches the food is the winner!

(They run back and forth. ABDAL *falls and starts to laugh.* HORTTEN *grabs the pot and eats from it. He turns his back to* ABDAL.*)*

ABDAL: *(Laughing)* I want some food! A couple of eggs! It's a new day! A couple of eggs to start the new day!

HORTTEN: I'll fry the eggs for you!

ABDAL: *(Struggling to get up)* No, I'll do it—I'll get up to do it.

HORTTEN: I'll fry the eggs for you—in bread! Ukrainian-style eggs in fried bread. You like that.

ABDAL: Yes, I like eggs in fried bread. Will you?

HORTTEN: Of course—of course!

ABDAL: *(In great despair)* I am a contraption with shoes! A square bundle! A person to ridicule! An ugly object!

*(*HORTTEN *fries eggs, smiles, and licks his fingers.)*

ABDAL: Soon I'll be deserted by everyone—alone...all alone! An object— that ejaculates! A fool! Why? Why?

HORTTEN: *(Bringing eggs to* ABDAL*)* Here are eggs and the bread is a nice color. Ukrainian-style eggs are good. *Bon appetit*, Abdal. Look at the sun, Abdal. What a wonderful color! Like your eggs. Swallow, chew, swallow but chew first...then swallow.

ABDAL: No, no, eggs will fall to the bottom of my buttocks. I'm too old to take chances with eggs. It might be my last meal. I'll be dead in the first decade of this century. I age so quickly. Bring me the empty pot. Let me bang it like a drum.

*(*HORTTEN *brings him the pot.)*

Hips and ass, poor dead Strauss, but-tocks and balls, procreating power, procreating power....Ah, if only I were young and in love with a beautiful lady—I would love her so much, I'd steal for her! Stuff food and bottles of wine, cakes, chocolate, stuff it all into my pockets! When I'd be in a store supposedly purchasing—I'd be stealing! Oooh I feel faint!

HORTTEN: Put your head between your knees—let the blood rush to it!

ABDAL: *(Bending over)* I smell an anal odor!

HORTTEN: *(Dancing)* I dance—I listen to the wind flowing through the grass! I make a lot of noise but in the end—

ABDAL: I fart!

HORTTEN: Stop your ridiculousness!

ABDAL: I'm a free man! You dance and sing! I listen to my own sound! I like all that is forbidden! To fart and murder! To blow Satan! To hate my enemy!

To torture...to torture...to bite the thigh of a beautiful woman! To go on the path of war with her! Twelve hours a day we'd make love! Swimming around in the holy of holies! Creating magnificent performances!... Do I look like a square bundle? A contraption with shoes! That ejaculates!

HORTTEN: No! No! Exploit your uniqueness! Make it marketable!

ABDAL: Marketable? My hips and ass?

HORTTEN: *(Laughing)* Two parts! Which came first—hips or ass? Does hunger exist without something that feeds? You know! Desires and impulses! The fake and the natural! Hairy balls! Perfumed pigs! All the world sleeping in the same position! Everything marketable!

ABDAL: I want a woman to make love with! To talk to at night! I want to squeeze a woman's wrists...to press her into the ground...to feel her wrap her legs around. *(He stares at* HORTTEN *and totters.)*

HORTTEN: Your hips and ass! Your grotesque body!

ABDAL: No, no—I'd have a beautiful body!

HORTTEN: When the cows come home! When Atlantis rises from the sea! When the Americans and the Chinese—

ABDAL: We'd swim the waves together! She'd touch my hands with love!

HORTTEN: *(Ironic)* Your love story is gripping me! Your vision—does she wear a silver shirt? Does your woman wear a silver shirt?

ABDAL: I don't know. Maybe, yes! Yes! She does!

HORTTEN: Are her breasts the right size? Not too big not too tiny.

ABDAL: They're small like an angel's!

HORTTEN: Angels are men! Boys!

ABDAL: Well, like a statue of a young girl! A pure ebony statue!

HORTTEN: Wowwowwowow!

ABDAL: Her mouth is trembling! Her nails dig—

HORTTEN: Into your hips and ass! And then—

ABDAL: She groans and moans—

HORTTEN: She giggles like a laundrywoman!

ABDAL: She gives me an ear bite!

HORTTEN: And lays an egg like a turtle!

ABDAL: A slim field marshal...and a lovely girl. I'm a slim field marshal with a lovely girl.

(ABDAL's dream vision of a handsome man in uniform and a young girl actualizes. They romantically dance. The speech of the man is Middle-European. Like STRAUSS's accent it does not have to be authentic. Fake Dutch, perhaps.)

ABDAL: Beauty is a hand's length from us! The beauty! It's sacred! Hortten, look! Her hair! The girl's hair is hanging down and her arms are stretching out in passion!

(The handsome man turns to ABDAL angrily, and the girl holds the man's arm, coy and very feminine.)

RONALD: I'd like to strangle you! You fat old man!

(The girl laughs happily, and RONALD swoops her up in his arms as loud and thrilling church bells peal. He runs off with her.)

ABDAL: *(In anguish)* My heart is a cave of ice. Why? Why? The young god of sunset—why did he talk that way to me?

HORTTEN: The young man wanted to slay a dragon—a monster for his girl! You happened to be standing there.

ABDAL: They are together. He and she. Beauty, youth, sky, and earth. A look at them and you know that life is not only a dog feast!

HORTTEN: You were an old fat dog to him!

ABDAL: Flames radiated from their bodies! Eagles do not have his beauty! His strength! He ran off with her! His fragile, perfect lady of love—to set her down on the edge of the Indian Ocean! They will eat cold cracked lobster and the sunset will kiss their gleaming bodies! *(He weeps.)* Divinity...please...give me divinity...I want it.

(He clasps his hands in prayer. HORTTEN brings him a pot of food. ABDAL angrily pushes it away with his foot; the pot breaks and cuts ABDAL's foot. HORTTEN, with great kindness, wipes the wound with a cloth dampened with wine from a bottle.)

HORTTEN: *(Consoling)* Abdal, they have no bodies, the man and girl—they have no bodies...and they live on worms! And they will inherit the heaven of the Jews! *(Pause)* Do you feel relaxed?

ABDAL: *(Self-pitying)* They will eat cold cracked lobster!

HORTTEN: It will turn to red dust in their mouths!

ABDAL: She will throw her lovely, slender arms around his strong body. The nostrils of God will widen with envy—at their beautiful passion!

HORTTEN: Insects! They have the feelings of insects!

ABDAL: They will eat cold cracked lobster and drink white wine after making love and swimming in the Indian Ocean...cold cracked lobster...cold cracked lobster. With golden-tinged God's hands, he, the young man, will give to her, the lovely-shaped and smooth, warm woman, her wild brown hair tasting of salt, he will give to her the meat of the cold lobster...and she will pour him wine. *(Dutch accent.)* Gev mij vit vin! Gev mij vit vin!

HORTTEN: They will die of a fever because of the lobster! He will find out that she has the toes of a dog—that she is a liar! And has breasts that are flat ugly fish! And he will hate her!

ABDAL: *(Reflecting)* The ocean is so gentle...it makes the man and girl so sleepy. She gazes at the new ornament he has given her. Lightning bursts the purple-flower sky...!

HORTTEN: Big ass! Big ass! She found out that he has a rusty asshole!

ABDAL: How did she find out!

HORTTEN: Because he thrust his ass out at her and asked that she...asked that she...! *(He makes an obscene gesture.)*

ABDAL: You are grotesque! I'll make you spread your legs in fear...in fear.

(He rushes at HORTTEN. HORTTEN pushes ABDAL and he falls clumsily.)

HORTTEN: *(Kindly)* My friend, my friend—I'm sorry. Abdal, some places in the world are bare of grass and filthy...and screaming with flies. But our love gently glows—and sometimes it sputters like a chicken frying! *(Laughs)*

ABDAL: Could we have chicken, tomorrow? Could we have a chicken for our meal, tomorrow—in the evening? Half for you and half for me. Cold watermelon to wash it down. Round hard grapes to eat with chicken!

HORTTEN: Yes, yes. Let's watch the sunset and then go to sleep.

ABDAL: Hortten, I want to sit for a while. You sleep.

(HORTTEN goes to sleep. ABDAL speaks reflectively.)

She springs. No! One knee springs like a pretty rabbit on a feather bed. Her leg is beautiful. Both legs. *(Laughs)* Long. *(Pause)* He, the young man, so strong, so strong.

(ABDAL lies down and weeps a little. The young man and girl appear again.)

PIA: You and me.

RONALD: Kiss me, cookie! Mine cock is protruding!

PIA: *(Laughing)* So be it! So be it! Big ears! Big teeth! Creature! Creature!

RONALD: Kiss me. Is good? Is good? I vant us to climb the shtronk rope! *(They embrace.)* Cold cracked lobster, girlie. Gev mij vit vin! Gev mij vit vin!

(ABDAL giggles softly.)

PIA: Ah, the sunset is dripping like golden honey over us! Ah, my knees! Are they not beautiful?

RONALD: Ah yes! Yah! Yah!

PIA: Do you love me?

RONALD: Yah! Yah!

PIA: But...but!

RONALD: *(Kissing her)* Cracked lobster!

PIA: Let us watch the Indian Ocean! *(She gracefully runs from him.)*

RONALD: *(Running after her)* You have the toenails of an angel! You haf the toenails of an angel! You haf da toenails uff an angel!

(ABDAL sobs and laughs. CHEMIST appears and builds a fire. He demonstrates to ABDAL how to squat over the fire. ABDAL squats over the flames and screams like a glorious martyr, triumphantly.)

ABDAL: *(Screaming)* O this beautiful body! O this noble body!

(He falls in a faint. All the characters appear and surround the CHEMIST. The mood becomes festive and very light.)

CHEMIST: *(To audience)* See, there is no grief here! I forbid grief here! We put grief in a mudhole!

(A bear trots in.)

CHEMIST: Grief will never escape from the mudhole! There is abandonment here! And true love.

(The bear makes coital motions and everybody becomes passionate and excessive.)

CHEMIST: This life is deeply felt!....After you fall headfirst into the mud hole!...Or ride upward to the thunder on an eagle's neck! Birds will help a scared-shit man! They feel bad for a man sticking in a mud-hole! They help a man escape! *(Pause)* Beware of the fake! Deception! Deception is this! *(He tears away the front lower part of the bear and a chicken head hangs out. He points to the bear's face and rips it off)* This is no lip! This is a muzzle! A muzzle of a bear! An animal! Wild game! A beast to hunt up!

(HORTTEN wakes up.)

HORTTEN: Where is Abdal?

CHEMIST: He's sleeping.

HORTTEN: *(Pointing to the characters, audience)* Who are they?

CHEMIST: People.

HORTTEN: And the bear? Is he a person?

CHEMIST: No, he is different.

HORTTEN: Did the bear kill the chicken?

CHEMIST: Yes.

HORTTEN: Why?

CHEMIST: Because of hunger.

(FANCHAR *laughs.*)

HORTTEN: *(Flirting)* You beauty! What's so funny? Tell us—we all love to laugh!

(FANCHAR *does not answer.* HORTTEN *notices* ABDAL.)

HORTTEN: Is my friend, Abdal, dead?

CHEMIST: No, he's tired. He shattered many rocks to enlarge the desert. He's tired.

HORTTEN: He makes the desert bigger! How much sand does he make?

CHEMIST: Five buckets a day. Five!

HORTTEN: How is it that I didn't know that Abdal has a job like that?

CHEMIST: Ich wisse nicht.

HORTTEN: You speak German. Do you know about Mr Strauss?

CHEMIST: Lie down on your back!

HORTTEN: What do you say to me?

CHEMIST: Lie down on your back!

HORTTEN: I don't want to!

CHEMIST: Lie down on your back—it will be good for you!

HORTTEN: I know what's good for me! Lay on my back! Lay on my back! Your demands are crazy! Lay on my back—so you can jump on me! Spit on me! Or shit! Look at Abdal—maybe you drugged him! Maybe—

CHEMIST: *(Forcing* HORTTEN *down)* Everything will be all right!

HORTTEN: Don't abuse me! Don't hurt me! Leave me alone! Don't hurt me like you hurt Abdal!

(CHEMIST *tears off part of the bear's face and fits it over* HORTTEN's *face.*)

CHEMIST: Survival of the fittest!

HORTTEN: *(Screaming)* Survival of the fittest!

CHEMIST: *(Tearing off the bear's penis and attaching it to* HORTTEN's *nose)* The true length of poetry!

(*The others laugh.*)

CHEMIST: Never laugh at a man's indignity! His humiliation—his pain.

HORTTEN: You are hurting me!

CHEMIST: I'm hurting you! Someone hurts someone!

HORTTEN: Me! My spirit!

CHEMIST: Shame on me! And shame on you! (*He kicks* HORTTEN *in the rear end.*)

HORTTEN: (*Trying feebly to defend himself*) I'll kill you! I'll kill you! Abdal, help me! Help!

(FANCHAR *makes obscene sounds. The others begin to mock* HORTTEN.)

HORTTEN: Bitches! Cocksuckers! Traitors! Bitches! (*He runs off*)

ABDAL: (*Sitting up*) I'm sitting on top of such and such part of the world. (*He moves from side to side.*) My stomach swaying! My bladder full! My chest sore with the pressure of a woman!

CHEMIST: A woman, where? Abdal, where?

ABDAL: A woman! A woman who loves me!

CHEMIST: Where is the woman!

ABDAL: Go smear yourself! Your questions—I don't have to tell you anything! Look at me!...What you did to my body!

CHEMIST: Abdal, you'll go on forever!

ABDAL: I'll go on forever! Why! What am I for! A monastic life! I don't want it—a hundred mournful years!

CHEMIST: You're blowing things up—exaggerating! Abdal, you are the salt of the earth!

ABDAL: I am not the salt of the earth! I'm Abdal! I'm Abdal!

CHEMIST: And what do you want? Lotions, ointments, leather, meat—friendly faces?

ABDAL: No!...Just...just what am I!

CHEMIST: A wide-hipped man! Not just a wide-hipped man. But especially a wide-hipped man! A grand and big-hipped man! The biggest-hipped black man on earth!

ABDAL: Where is my woman?

CHEMIST: Rooting around...putting flowers behind her ears...stepping over...filth...pondering about your honor and self-sacrifice.

ABDAL: Like a martyr?

CHEMIST: Between the woman's legs—the gaping crevice!

ABDAL: My love! My love! She's little and beautiful!

CHEMIST: Very beautiful—like a tiger's tooth!

ABDAL: I would love to touch my woman!

CHEMIST: Death...death...death. Death before your eyes! *(He smiles.)*

ABDAL: You baloney! You morbid baloney!

CHEMIST: It is...holy...scripture.

ABDAL: What is! What's holy scripture!

CHEMIST: Your one-man plague!

ABDAL: My plague?

CHEMIST: *(Laughing)* Your plug!

ABDAL: My plug?

CHEMIST: No, Abdal! Your one-man plague! The plug is nothing!

ABDAL: You baloney! You crazy baloney! You crazy liar!

CHEMIST: I'm like an open bag...just an open bag—and life and death pours out. *(Laughs)*

ABDAL: Pour your spleen out! Where's Hortten! Where's my friend!

CHEMIST: *(Laughing)* Hortten! Hortten! Plunge into a hole—with fat!

ABDAL: Plunge into a hole with fat—plunge into a hole with fat! Strauss said that!

CHEMIST: When he had living eyes and a mouth.

ABDAL: You baloney! You judge! You trickster!

(ABDAL *lunges at the* CHEMIST. CHEMIST *hurls him down.*)

CHEMIST: Hunger...hunger...hunger.

ABDAL: Hunger! Eat the cheese from a dog's vomit!

CHEMIST: I'll remove your fingers and you will only have a thumb on each hand!

ABDAL: No! No! No! Where is Hortten, where's Hortten!

CHEMIST: He is tanning hides.

(HORTTEN *appears.*)

ABDAL: I was calling and calling you. I didn't know that you tanned hides!

CHEMIST: The potatoes are burning!

ABDAL: Are there potatoes? I'll save them. *(He comes back with potatoes.)* Here, Hortten, my friend. Eat some potato!

HORTTEN: Scrape the skin away for me, please.

ABDAL: You, a tanner of hides! And I should remove the skin of a potato for you!

HORTTEN: I want it that way.

(ABDAL *peels a potato and hands it to* HORTTEN. *They eat and the* CHEMIST *watches them.*)

CHEMIST: It...is...said....

ABDAL: *(Absently)* What is said?

HORTTEN: *(Laughing)* Yes, what is said?

CHEMIST: It is said of Abdal and Hortten that they were born again!

ABDAL: *(Laughing)* If this is my life—then stuff me back in an old grave mound! *(Disgust)* This is my life!

HORTTEN: It ain't bad now with potatoes. *(Laughs)*

ABDAL: Potatoes aren't everything!

CHEMIST: *(Intensely)* It is said of Abdal and Hortten that they were born again!

ABDAL: *(Cheerfully)* We heard you, we heard you. Hortten, look, the magician has fire in his eyes!

HORTTEN: *(Eating)* Yes—I see. *(Pause)* Abdal, why do men in armor eat raw meat? It's a joke, a riddle joke. Do you know the answer?

ABDAL: Meat! If we had some meat with the potatoes!

HORTTEN: Men in armor eat raw meat—because they only boil for war! *(Laughs)* Get it! Abdal, do you get it!

ABDAL: *(Icily)* Yes...I...got...it!

HORTTEN: They only boil for war—they leap on dead flesh!

ABDAL: Fleisch!

HORTTEN: What?

ABDAL: Fleisch? Flesh? Fleisch?

HORTTEN: Bleeding heart! *(Mocking* ABDAL*)* Softie! You're thinking about the laundryman again! Strauss! Strauss! Whenever you speak a foreign word, a German word—it's because of Strauss!

CHEMIST: It is said of Abdal and Hortten—that they were born again!

ABDAL: You're eating all the potatoes, Hortten! Give me that last one!

HORTTEN: I need my strength up, Abdal! Let me have it!

ABDAL: I want it! My frame needs flesh! I have a big frame!

HORTTEN: I need the energy! I want the potato!

ABDAL: Bastard! You ate all the spuds!

HORTTEN: Not all the spuds! Not all!

ABDAL: Give me that spud! Give me the potato!

HORTTEN: I need it! I need it! The potato! The spud! I need it more than you!

ABDAL: My frame is larger! Bigger! I'm a heavy fella!

(HORTTEN *angrily chews up some potato and spits it at* ABDAL.)

ABDAL: Spit your swill at me will you! Spit your swill at me! *(He pushes* HORTTEN'*s face into the potato.)*

HORTTEN: Square ass! Square ass! Ugly black square ass! Contraption! Cripple! Cripple—murderer!

(*The* CHEMIST *causes a snake to drop on* ABDAL. *He becomes rigid with fear.)*

HORTTEN: *(Tenderly and calmly holding his arms out to* ABDAL *and singing)*
Wash baby's hands
And wash baby's head,
Dry him and comb his hair.
Tell him to sleep in peace.
Let bygones be bygones, friend. Of all things, what I love most is our friendship! *(He grabs the snake off* ABDAL'*s fear-rigid body.)* Let's slice a snake up!

ABDAL: *(Gasping his relief)* Let bygones be bygones! Yes! Yes! Let bygones be bygones! We slice a snake up! That's what we'll do! *(Joking, pretending.)* . But Abdal doesn't know where we can get a snake!

HORTTEN: We'll find one! We'll find one! We're not that unlucky!

(*He pulls a knife out of his pocket and cuts the snake in half. They both take turns slicing the snake up and eating the pieces.)*

ABDAL: Fleisch! Fleisch! Fleisch! Ist goot! Ist goot! Any more potato?

HORTTEN: Gone—all gone! Like your victim!

ABDAL: Who?

HORTTEN: Your victim! Strauss! Strauss! Y'gawdamn louse!

ABDAL: *(Clutching his belly in pain)* O Adam! Solomon! Samson and David! Saint Julian! Julian! Julian! O Lord Jesus!

HORTTEN: You've got a stomach ache, you glutton! You ate all the potatoes! All the snake meat! You can thank your own greed!

ABDAL: It's my heart! It's my heart! I'm dying!

HORTTEN: When you die it will be doomsday!

ABDAL: *(Belching)* Better...better... *(Belching)* better...better!

HORTTEN: The glutton says better...better...better...betterbetterbetter!
(To audience.) I wish I was friendless! I wish I never knew Abdal! Why!
Why! I'm blameless! Blameless!

(ABDAL belches.)

HORTTEN: Lord, how can I make use of this circumstance! Why did you
betray my noble spirit! Why have I fallen out of high degree into this
misery! Why am I with this false-ass! Is he my evil judgment! This foul
friendship! Lord, when wilt thou find me a good friend for my need!
A true and good friendship! O Lord, I crave it—I crave it!

ABDAL: *(Going to* HORTTEN—*embracing him)* Friend, I'm better! I'm better,
Abdal is better! I can even sing a song. *(He sings a refrain of* Greensleeves.)
Hortten, let's make up a game! Tell me a story! Make up a song! Brag to
me! Boast! I want you to be in a good mood! Shall I make up a poem, a new
poem? We'll play! Play! Make up a new song? Do you hate me? No! I'm
Abdal! We've had our quarrels! We've given each other runs for our money!
I'm glad to have had a good run for the money! *(He pulls some potatoes out of
his clothes.)* Here, Hortten, potatoes! More potatoes! I'll juggle! Let's both
juggle!

*(HORTTEN is silent and morose. ABDAL steps backward and looks surprised as he
realizes he has just stepped on a sleeping bag with a pair of lovers inside.*

ABDAL: Love! Love! Love! The link to magic and the cosmos!
(He feels the bag.) The combat! Did you do the combat?
Who holds who? Does boy hold girl or does girl hold boy?
Do both hug each other in the delightful game? I toss flowers! I toss flowers
and poetry at you!

(Gun and explosion sounds)

ABDAL: War is here! War is here! Bloody violence! Do your stuff, you lovers,
before you die! Come on! Play! Combat! Mingle your wetness!

*(The sleeping bag is perfectly still; the heads of the lovers are exposed and the faces
have a frozen look of passion.)*

ABDAL: Come on! Come on! Be the tender barbarians with each other! Kiss!
Bite! Suck! Fornicate! Commit the sweet ordeal! The touch of the sweetest
feeling! The feeling of the sweetest touch! Breathe at each other! Snort in
each other's faces. Bump your asses together! *(To* HORTTEN.) He pries her
jaws open! She pries his jaws open! They are both seventeen! He will die in
the war! And she the lovely maid like a hinge flying off a gate will fly to his
memory over and over. The memory of her seventeen-year-old lover who
had his beautiful young life evilly tricked by death into nothingness—just
the stickiness of drying ooze of blood and sperm and mucus. Death—death
like the white, white finger of a politician! *(He emits a high screech.)* The white

finger! *(To the sleeping bag.)* Does your pussy tingle with passion? Your groins? Your groins? I am very serious! Lovemaking is more precious than goldmaking! Spielen ein spiel, hoop de hoop bop de bop hoy moy toy poloy! Win! Win! Buttocks balls birds arrows lips sinews oceans teeth rabbits big eyes! Big ears! Big-footed singing crying vomiting and shining sharp-elbowed lightning killing grieving lovers! Lovers! Lovers! Speak to me! Speak! *(He jumps on the bag.)* Frauds! Traitors! *(He pulls at the two heads and they come off in his hands.)* Wow! Wow! Wow! Who can do that? Who can do what I can do! Grab and get! Grab and get! Heads! Heads! What a wondrous thing is man! I am on the warpath! You cannot fight me! I carry you! Like a bundle! You sweet lovers! Sweet, sweet lovers! Kiss! Kiss! *(He rubs the two heads together.)* Tremblers! Consumers! Pleasure angels! Plug up! Plug up! You pluggers of holes! Birds will sing their joy at your day of love! And I'll sing a German song!

(A volume of birdsong is heard. FANCHAR *appears and sits. She is majestic. Her four men—*BROWD, EDGAHL, HAMFER, *and* STARKLED*—attempt ritualistically to pull her knees apart.* FANCHAR's *face is serene. The knees give way and civilization gives way. The men are cold and bloodless in the denigrating act on* FANCHAR. *Whenever her knees are forced apart,* ABDAL *screams.)*

ABDAL: Eli Eli lama sabacthani! Eli Eli lama sabacthani!

(Blackout. Time passes.)

(HORTTEN *and* ABDAL *are together.)*

ABDAL: I would have killed those violators!

HORTTEN: Why didn't you?

ABDAL: What do you say!

HORTTEN: Why didn't you kill them! The violators!

ABDAL: Let's stop this! Let's stop this! Questions! I'm tired! *(Pause)* Are you calling me a coward?

HORTTEN: *(Picking up a potato)* I love the steam from the potato!

ABDAL: Make the crack bigger!

HORTTEN: The crack in the potato? Why?

ABDAL: So the steam will come out! *(Laughs)*

HORTTEN: You're a bad fellow! I think that I've had my fill of you. *(Pause)* I'm only joking, Abdal. But someplace else, somewhere else you would have died for what you did—or didn't do! Not protecting the woman from the violators!

ABDAL: *(Mimicking)* Not protecting the woman from the violators!

HORTTEN: There's no use for a coward in this world!

ABDAL: Fat white duck! I laid Fanchar—you are jealous! I laid the beautiful woman! I laid the beautiful woman! I felt her teeth dig into my neck! Oh, it was good! She bit me like a dog! Harder, harder! She screamed, harder! Harder! Her ass was burning like a rabbit on the fire! I chewed her hair! We made love four days straight! I chewed her like a wad of tobacco! I dived into her like a turkey buzzard into a hen! She grabbed my pecker with her trap! And my pecker turned into a horn of bronze!

HORTTEN: Gold is more precious, false-ass!

ABDAL: Bronze is the metal of justice!

HORTTEN: *(Mimicking)* Justice! Justice! Turkey-foot!

ABDAL: Turkey-foot your ass!

HORTTEN: Bragging! Bragging about fornication! A dream of fornication!

ABDAL: Hortten, what is the air? What is the tongue? What is play? *(He dances around* HORTTEN.*)*

HORTTEN: Don't you come close to me—your body has a stink!

ABDAL: *(Cheerfully)* Like ripening crops! I smell like ripening crops! That's good. Very good! Holy! Sacred! Holy! Sacred! I'm a heavy piece of meat! Flesh! Flesh! I'm sacred! Sacred! I feel the deity in me!

HORTTEN: *(Mockingly)* Bundle! The bundle feels the deity in him!

ABDAL: Hortten, we will fast! Yes! We will fast! It will be beneficial for the heart and soul! My head is full of the thought of contamination! You, Hortten, are contaminated! A little putrid! We will fast! Beneficial, yes, beneficial for the soul!

HORTTEN: *(Angrily)* The bunghole also!

ABDAL: Also the bunghole!

HORTTEN: I will not fast! Never! Never!

ABDAL: You will fast! You fool!

HORTTEN: *(Laughing)* Look! Look! The bundle calls a man a fool! He can only ejaculate! The bundle that ejaculates calls a man a fool! A freak in the world of nature! *(He picks up some red mud and throws it at* ABDAL.*)* You look like you're bleeding!

(Pause. ABDAL *wipes mud away.)*

ABDAL: You, Hortten, look...like a putrid corpse, dug up! A putrid corpse dug up!

HORTTEN: What a terrible thing to say to me! Bleeding freak!

ABDAL: Geezer! Geezer! Putrid geezer! Corpse of contamination!

HORTTEN: Bundle! Bundle! You're going to die!

ABDAL: *(Running)* That's what you think! I can run fast! Faster than death!
You will die! Not Abdal! See! See! How fast I can run! See! See! I run! I play
a run! I run for real! *(He runs wildly around* HORTTEN.*)* I outrun the fuckers
who run! I run on your heart! Your liver! Your balls! I shame you into a
feeble halt! My great and mighty running! My great and mighty running
shames you! I run agilely like a swift and beautiful king! I am a king! I run
up the water tower! *(He attempts to run up the tower but can't and starts to
climb.)* Give me the assbone! Give me the assbone, Hortten! The assbone!

(HORTTEN hands him a bone.)

HORTTEN: Nut! Nut! Nut! I'm playing with you! Humoring you!

ABDAL: The assbone! I have the assbone! With it—the assbone! This assbone!
I will pierce the mystery of God! *(He starts to lose his balance.)* I will pierce!
I will! I will scratch! *(He falls and lies still.)*

HORTTEN: Abdal! Good Abdal! My friend! Friend! Don't play this way,
my Abdal! Do you live? Are you alive? Bundle! Hey bundle! Get up, you're
made of iron! O my beloved false-ass, get up! You're frightening me! O K?
Scaring me? O K? I'll kick your rear! False-ass! Abdal, my beloved friend!
Sweet sweet brother! Bastard—you're tricking me! You're trying to trick me!
You snake in the grass! You false-assed snake in the grass! Don't trick me!
Buffoon! Buffoon! Don't trick me! Louse! Trickster! Trickster! Get up!
Stop hoodwinking me! Stop! Stop—you're depriving me...of my of my...!
You're not dead! You're immortal! Listen! I was kind to you! If you lie here
too long—rats will gnaw your eyes out! I think we should fast! Yes! Yes!
We should fast! I'm overstuffed! Your idea about fasting is good!

(ABDAL ascends to heaven. HORTTEN watches amazed, screams.)

HORTTEN: What about the summertime! Big hips! The summertime!
We're supposed to be together in the summer! My love! We were supposed
to fish together! You like broiled split fish! Come down to me! Come down
to me! There's nothing up there! In the sky! I should have nailed you down!
I should have nailed your body down—you wouldn't have left me!
Glorious Abdal...my friend! Possessor of the sweet night! Come down
to me...I'm begging you! Abdal! Abdal! I'll bring water! I'll bring oil!
Abdal...come down to me! Come down to me!

END OF PLAY

THREE FRONT

ORIGINAL PRODUCTION

THREE FRONT was first produced at the Omaha Magic Theater, opening on 25 November 1988. The cast and creative contributors were:

EVELYN ....JoAnn Schmidman
BUSH W .... William York Hyde
NITA & TANYA .... Margie Du Be

Stage directions ....The Company
Flute ....Catherine Berg, Shuli Rayberg
Synthesizers & sound effects .... Catherine Berg
Percussion .... John J Sheehan
Images . . . . . .Sora Kim, Phyllis Kohl, Barb Loper, Shuli Rayberg, Roger Reeves

Director ....JoAnn Schmidman
Designer ....Sora Kim & JoAnn Schmidman
Lighting .... Matt Irvin
Piano .... Rick Hiatt
Graphics design .... Michael Franks & the Graphix Group
Public relations ....Rose Marie Whitely

CHARACTERS & SETTING

EVELYN: *attractive, strong. She is in her forties or fifties.*
BUSH W: *her husband. Energetic and successful businessman.*
NITA: *his assistant. Good-looking, strong, she could be Asian but not necessarily.*
   EVELYN'*s lover.*
TANYA: *a prostitute. Slight accent. The role is played by the actress who plays* NITA.

A dank office trailer. Outside. A room in a house. A hotel lounge. The set should be a maximum of simplicity, meant only to 'represent' symbolically.

The locales are a city in America and one in Thailand, plus Salzburg. The lighting might be considered the most important single element in a series of changing scenes and flashbacks that fuse the past and present.

The play is about people living at the extremes of experience. It is told as much by its imagery and the sound values of the dialogue as it is by its plot.

ACT ONE

Scene One

(Outside. A dank office trailer, to the side of the trailer, sticking above the ground is a hose fixed to a hole leading to an abandoned coal mine. BUSH W is watching his assistant NITA vainly trying to revive a truck driver who lies on the ground.)

BUSH: Is the fella coming to?! Is he coming around?!

NITA: He's unconscious because of the fumes! He must get to a hospital! You call!

BUSH: I can't! I just can't! You work on him some more! Work on him!

NITA: He's dead! He asphyxiated because of the toxic fumes.

BUSH: Dead? This one has messed us up. Dead!

NITA: *(Seething)* Won't you call the hospital?! You ought to call!

BUSH: Yesterday, the mine overflowed. It's a criminal offense! Besides he's already...gone. *(Righteous)* It's not easy being a toxic waste entrepreneur! The shortage of available legal sites. Midnight dumping expeditions! One of your drivers dead.

NITA: *(Angry)* It's a criminal offense.

BUSH: Now, you know that I don't like that terminology—criminal offense!

NITA: You yourself said it! The toxic waste poured into the river—into the town's water supply.

BUSH: A helluva sight. Frankly, I find it difficult to believe. Well, it's too late to do anything about it. Now, for some teamwork! We'll bury him together.

NITA: If you like.

BUSH: *(Courtly)* Well, you know that I'd like that very much.

(Lights fade. A rain storm starts up. Inside the trailer BUSH pours coffee out of a thermos bottle into a cut-glass cup.)

BUSH: Everything that has ever interested me has come my way. Oblivion waits.

NITA: *(Angry)* What the fuck does that mean?!

BUSH: It's the storm...utter freedom.

NITA: *(Sarcastic)* Rain bounces endlessly irregularly limitless dimensions blind energy. A sign of strength.

BUSH: That's right. You understand.

NITA: The damn rain makes me paranoid.

BUSH: It's your bad nerves. You have lots of pressure and lots of authority. I'm awfully grateful to you. You are the one who manages to make us come out ahead in virtually every deal we make. You know that.

NITA: You better believe it.

BUSH: When the department of environmental resources was tipped off about the illegal dumping you acted like the spill was a tremendous shock to you! You were incredible—brilliant! *(Singing)*
There ain't no flies on us!
There ain't no flies on us!
There might be flies
On the other guys but there
Ain't no flies on us!

NITA: *(Cynical)* Just standard business practice in an unglamorous business. Grimy trucks—vile liquids—altered chromosomes—deformed fetuses.

BUSH: Now don't you be provocative! No moral tones! Especially in this downpour! It does nobody any good.

NITA: *(In a burst)* Like learning the Thai language! What good does it do if you're not in Thailand!

BUSH: Your bad nerves! Do neck exercises! It'll relax the muscles. I know a good masseuse.

NITA: People have a right to normal every day life. Don't they?

BUSH: *(Exasperated)* Now, you don't sound like my equal! You're trying to convince me of something. That's a dead-end.

(NITA rubs her neck.)

BUSH: See! Muscle strain! Neck exercise! Do it! Like young people say— just hang loose!

NITA: You hang loose! *(Exploding)* Three years ago, in Thailand I had a fling with a successful businessman's wife!

BUSH: *(Ironic)* Oh, you are shocking me. Did you go dancing with her? As if I don't know what you are—a greedy woman.

NITA: Passionately in love with your wife.

BUSH: *(Somberly)* So be it.

NITA: How could I ever win. You weaken us!

BUSH: Truth weakens you. Isn't it wonderful?! It gives a deep sense to life. You see the way back to your own beginning.

NITA: Yes...thoughts are bound to death. A woman never descends so deep as when she does not know where she's going.

BUSH: I told you—no gloom! *(Reflective)* You know, when I first met Evelyn I also knew she was a rare woman—she moved like an athlete—strong firm legs.

NITA: There's a dead man lying in the rain...lying near a hose on the poisonous ground.

BUSH: Now, why don't you just go ahead and set those words to music— be a protest folk-singer! *(Laughs)*

NITA: *(Reflective)* Coldness of the skin...rigidity of body muscles...bluish discoloration of the face and lips...the horror and danger finished.

BUSH: *(Gently)* Change happens in this little world of ours, Nita. The atoms in the universe bounce up against each other in a ballet—just like a ballet of constant motion—like the rain. *(Pause)* We gave him artificial respiration! We tried! We tried! We wanted him to stop dying. He wouldn't.

NITA: *(Coldly)* If one is to be paid exceedingly well for being a murderer, well why not be a murderer? *(Explodes)* Bush W, do you know that one of your eyes is slightly higher than the other?

BUSH: Your talk reminds me of a woman hallucinating.

NITA: I have a better memory than you.

BUSH: *(Disgust)* Thanks to you my wife became a pervert.

NITA: Can't you let us live?

BUSH: *(Angry)* I am a vital man! I am larger than you! Shall I continue, Ms? I have the balls and you will wallow in envy! *(Calm)* To give care, to protect—and to guarantee the reproduction of the species are sacred responsibilities.

NITA: *(Contempt)* Real good barbecue sauce. Bush W's sweet and sour.

BUSH: I make the basic rules. I will tell the tale. Evelyn my wife will beg for my blessing one day.

NITA: And the day after—what then?

BUSH: Now, you and I are part of a team. *(Indignant)* We are not part of a criminal element. Are our files in order?

NITA: *(Clipped tones)* Right as rain. All our files are clean. All incriminating documents have been—

BUSH: *(Excited)* Go ahead—say it! Shredded! Shredded! Boy, I like that word! Shredded! What a neat idea! And you masterminded it!

NITA: I became absorbed in the responsibility.

BUSH: Exactly! It happens that way. And always think of yourself as a hero and a patriot! You know, Nita, you and I have a natural exuberance! We've got to express it.

NITA: *(Reflective)* In Thailand Evelyn noticed that about me—my hunger.

BUSH: From one day to the next is the most difficult to endure—for all of us. *(Kindly)* Be patient. Don't try to rebel so much. You have authority.

NITA: As much as a...severed hand.

BUSH: Just one day to live. And questions—what injures me? What injures us all? The point is not to disappear—

NITA: *(Pointing outside)* Like him!

BUSH: Be a reasonable woman! Like the atoms—you'll never stop—I'll never stop! *(Controlled)* What's the worst thing that can happen to you in this place—this dank trailer—paper cuts? Getting your hand caught in the Xerox rollers? Look! There's no blood on the floor! Remember—just each day to live—to live—to thrive! Thrive!

(Lights fade to blackness.)

Scene Two

(In Thailand. The first meeting. The mood is romantic. There is a camera and equipment lying about.)

EVELYN: Regrets? If I ever had them looking at you, now, I've forgotten them. You were the one who wanted me to take you to America. I didn't ask you. I never could have asked you. You know that I have a husband. I can see him coming out of the house, squinting in the sunlight, the rage cramping his jaw. He's waiting for my memorable return. I wanted him to come with me to Thailand. "How can I live there, he said." I wanted us to take the trip together, to be together. But I enjoy traveling alone and I love this land. I love the people, the rivers, the forests, the rich black earth. We should take each step as if it were the last. We don't know where we are going to die. Like poets we should sing praises to the loveliness of young girls, the worship of nature, the love of innocence in nature. Beauty appears fresh, delicate and surprising. Our first duty is to avoid the falsity as best we can, no matter what its form. Woman like fire and water makes the truth live within herself. We must go beyond everything there is in the world. To love you was to bring myself to another realm. *(Pause)* It's astonishing to be here in the only country in southeast Asia never taken over by a European power! It belongs to itself—this country.

NITA: It was the Queen and her daughter in the early part of the century. They were strong and lucky.

EVELYN: I'm glad that you're going to America with me. You'll have to adjust to the chill of autumn. We'll sit in front of a crackling fire on a stone hearth, look out of the windows framing the rust and gold of trees. A home is made of love alone. I'll knit you a beautiful warm sweater and tuck a patchwork quilt around you. We'll drink steaming mugs of hot buttered rum. I'll teach you how to cook a traditional Sunday dinner. A succulent roast beef. *(Poetic)* Choice viands and a skillful cook invite the puny and capacious appetite. Then let politeness, joined to hunger, haste and learn the method how to dine in taste.

NITA: *(Urgent tone)* You like me...don't you?

EVELYN: *(Teasing)* No, you're disgusting. I despise you. I will make a monkey out of you if you don't fall into step. You like me, don't you? Everything shows on your face!

NITA: I would like to hear you say—

EVELYN: What?! What?! That you excite me?! Yes! You excite me—your hunger, your yearnings. Happy now?

NITA: I'm very attracted to you. *(She starts to set up the photo equipment.)*

EVELYN: Because I'm the first woman who seduced you. We only know each other for two weeks. You're a sleeping beauty. I am one who love inspires like a leaf on a branch which goes away and another comes.

NITA: This is a good time for me. There are no claims on me.

EVELYN: But I'm all tangled impulses. I am not resigned and detached. I am selfish and I want devotion. A sacred respect. You must believe in me. We will thrive and prosper. A home is made of love alone. You will bring your cares to me. You and I in every pose, sexual, tender, our hands and teeth, our noses close together. And I will hold your curving body taut with desire.

(Lights fade to blackness.)

Scene Three

(Inside the trailer. BUSH is looking over some folders. NITA enters.)

BUSH: Have my drivers come? My worker bees? My drones?

NITA: Not yet.

BUSH: It's past twelve! They're late! Nita, there is one who appreciates classical music. I even discussed Mahler with him, and the Salzburg festival—and baseball! (*Laughs*)

NITA: Which one?

BUSH: His name is Pete. He has a crippled son, and a daughter. I was really surprised when I discovered that Pete is not intellectually impoverished like the others. He's a sensitive fella. He told me that he has an autographed baseball used by the 1952 Brooklyn Dodgers! I like talking to my drivers, occasionally, about their lives. I show concern for them and interest. It's a way of finding out who is likely to be susceptible to emotional stress. Those are the dangerous ones.

NITA: The ones to be watched.

BUSH: Yes. They're the ones who are likely to upset people's way of life.

NITA: And their economic interests.

BUSH: You bet your sweet ass. (*Suspicious*) You don't ever discuss our business with Evelyn?!

NITA: Your enthusiasm for covert operations? I don't.

BUSH: Evelyn couldn't understand. Don't you know?

NITA: I know.

BUSH: (*Slyly*) We've dumped millions of gallons of hazardous waste illegally into the city's landfills and sewers. It's better than sex! (*Laughs*) Hah! I knew you'd like that!

NITA: (*Musing*) What of the mother who seeks her dead child on the riverbank?

BUSH: One day this operation will help with the cleanup—

NITA: Hypocrite! You don't see the beauty or the fragility of the land.

BUSH: Now, see here, woman! We are a team! There's money in the bank for everyone on the team! You take responsibility ! Enjoy it! It's authentic experience!

NITA: Yes. Of course.

BUSH: That's right. I live like any successful business executive. Expensive cars, yachts and a vacation home—and a wife who makes—pilgrimages to Asia!

NITA: On her next trip she wants me with her. (*She exits.*)

BUSH: We'll see. (*Jovial*) Is this not wonderful? This secret trailer. And from our union crime is born!

(*The sound of oncoming trucks*)

BUSH: My drivers have come! My worker bees! They're late! They're supposed to pick up the waste oil and sludge at midnight! Who's fucking off? I own two dozen trucks. I operate under as many as eight different corporate names! The drivers don't have the slightest notion how difficult it is to stay in this business! Not an altruist among them, Har! har! har! Lowlife, I'll give them some hazardous material up the ass. Slovenly bunch overloaded the dumping site—that's why one of the jokers died! I take all the risks! You save your ass I save mine. Shaft me shaft thee! My sincerest desire is to do damage! And get away with my cock and balls. Sincerity and rectitude that's my game—har!!! I keep pace with the modern world. Three million years ago, a robust species of man, taller and heavier than Hah!—their competitors—made tools! Made of stone and animal bones! Miraculous! Precious knowledge, agriculture, civilization, god-like power! Chemical waste alters chromosomes and deforms fetuses. If my wife had a turkey in the oven I'd give her bottled water to drink, Har! Har! Midnight dumping expeditions, it's not an easy way to make a living. Drivers! Villains! Where art thou! When thy horns honk my bones clank! Don't torment me with thy lateness! Drive your black horses furious through this criminal night! Squeeze my righteousness hard! Let us join together our shuddering loins and dump on the city! Midnight pollutions! The earth swallows! The night is lonely without my drivers! Heart in my hands I wait for thy haulers! Come boys! Fly thy suicide missions! Grovel beside the hose, bow your heads at the dumpsite and crow!

(Lights fade to blackness.)

Scene Four

(A room in a house. EVELYN is sitting on an elegant settee. BUSH stands nearby. They avoid looking at each other directly, only seeing each other with vague side-long glances. The tonal qualities of their speech creates a repressed and sinister effect.)

EVELYN: Well, if you won't go with me to Thailand this time, let Nita come. I know she's your right hand. I need her too, though.

BUSH: Why, my dear?

EVELYN: *(Stammers)* I-I-I-I want h-h-h-her to go with me to Thailand.

BUSH: *(Patronizing)* Bless you dear, I feel pulled and tugged to let you have her.

EVELYN: We'll go then?

BUSH: *(Pause)* My dear, a minor crisis occurred. A matter of business.

EVELYN: *(Urgent)* Let it wait!

BUSH: My dear, you know I'd rather not do that.

EVELYN: Oh well, couldn't you?!

BUSH: A crisis, dear.

EVELYN: Oh well, I did hope. *(Laughs)*

BUSH: Is something funny, dear?

EVELYN: It was just a thought...something I remembered.

BUSH: You remembered a funny thought. I'll give you a penny for it, dear. *(He removes a penny from his pocket and forces it into her rigid hand.)* Tell me.

EVELYN: I was thinking of Hummingbird pattern wallpaper. *(Pause)* People who are not used to fine things and unsure of their taste never make the right choices.

BUSH: Confusing issues again, dear? Waxing poetic? What's going on in that little head? Tell me. I don't want to be left behind.

EVELYN: Well, I thought of the mansion that Nita and I visited in Thailand. The dining room was covered with Hummingbird pattern wallpaper. We had such a time trying to count the birds.

BUSH: What else did you do, dear?

EVELYN: We met a lot of young people. And we had a rowboat outing. There was so much goodwill.

BUSH: I'm glad.

EVELYN: I was sorry to leave. *(Pause)* Oh well, it's important to preserve a memory.

BUSH: Dear, of course. Memory makes very little demand of us. What else?

EVELYN: Well, I had a kind of...tranquility.

BUSH: And you were sorry to lose it?

EVELYN: I think so. How did you know that?

BUSH: *(Jovial)* I calculated it, dear. I'm a businessman. Of all the things to do with yourself, what makes the right sense now?

EVELYN: *(Urgent)* Let Nita come with me, please!

BUSH: Your life isn't organized, Evelyn.

EVELYN: Please! Please! Please!

BUSH: *(Tremulous, feigning pity)* I can't. I just can't.

EVELYN: Please, we want to—

BUSH: No, dear. It's only you who wants to.

EVELYN: *(Resigned)* Alright. Perhaps this is not the appropriate time.

BUSH: No—not the appropriate time.

EVELYN: I'll go alone.

BUSH: Dear, my dear, sweetie, sweetie, you go, you go.

(EVELYN exits. Telephone rings and BUSH answers it.)

BUSH: *(Pause)* Yes, Pete. I'm always interested in good ideas. And I reward cooperation. I think you can do a first-rate job on all of this. There are opportunities here for all of us. I hope you'll take advantage of them. *(Pause)* Now Pete, you must understand that it would be best for the whole family if you sent your boy to a school equipped to deal with his disabilities. *(Pause)* Of course you'll miss him, that's natural. But you'll get up in the morning, you'll go to work, you'll eat your dinner. You'll work smoothly, efficiently, quietly. *(Laughs)* I prefer the other man's conflict! Now, stress will undermine your health. That special school, it's still the best hope. You can count on me like a brother to remind you of your duties... or to scourge you with criticism. Pete, be like me. Keep yourself busy with the tasks of community life. But don't forget to get the show on the road if you know what I mean. The long haul. I'm not sure it's moving as quickly as I'd like it to move. Be like me—try to make the birds fly backwards. That's right—make 'em fly backwards. That's the secret of success. Well, I consider myself a team-builder.

(Black-out)

(EVELYN and NITA are together.)

EVELYN: He should die! Die! Die! For not letting you go with me! He's our destroyer! He eats up all the air! We're his victims! And you offer up anything and everything to him! You're his lackey!

NITA: His assistant!

EVELYN: His assistant! You're pitiful. He gets what he wants out of you.

NITA: I get what I want.

EVELYN: I get what I want! You even emulate him! What do you get?

NITA: What's the matter, Evelyn? Are we mismated?

EVELYN: You're devoted to him! He's so charming and doting!

NITA: We're mismatched! Mismated! You should divorce me.

(EVELYN attempts to strike her but is physically restrained by her.)

EVELYN: Nita is a cheater! Nita is a cheater! Piker! Piker! Piker!

NITA: You knew I had a focused mission from the very beginning! Remember! I still do. You admired my masculine virtues!

EVELYN: I wanted you to go with me to Thailand! That's all I wanted! But you want to pick our eyes out! *(She exits.)*

NITA: I'm also alone in the world. That still isn't a reason for me to follow you to a jungle in Thailand! I don't share your obsessions. They are not mine. Your intellect! My hands, they look ugly, cruel. I feel contempt for one and hate the other. All the chaos under the surface of things. Will I kill people and send them to the glue factory? Yes, Evelyn, I followed you. You didn't drag me here. And I told you that I remember you saying that we will give each other scented soap and praise. *(Pause)* One day we will watch Bush W shove the tips of his fingers into his mouth and bite on them—with our hands we will grip his jaws together until the tears roll down his cheeks!

(Lights fade to blackness.)

(Lights up. One month later. Visual image of a woman with explosives strapped to her body. EVELYN and NITA are sitting together.)

EVELYN: The return flight was unbelievable! A nightmare! A woman hijacker no less! She said that she had explosives strapped to her body. She threatened to blow up the plane!

NITA: Bush W wished that she had. He told me that as we listened to the news report of the hijacking.

EVELYN: *(Ignoring the comment)* She threatened to blow us all up unless she received three hundred thousand dollars and her child to be flown from Europe to Thailand!

NITA: She was right.

EVELYN: Right about what?

NITA: She was right to act upon her desperation.

EVELYN: She said that she no longer felt thirst or hunger. It didn't do her any good. They locked her up and threw away the key. *(Laughs)*

NITA: Didn't anybody try to do something?

EVELYN: A man began to yell insults! We made him shut up. We didn't want her to blow up the plane because of that idiot!

NITA: Maybe, all together you could have disarmed her.

EVELYN: I told you the explosives were strapped to her body.

NITA: You might have tried! ·

EVELYN: Luckily we didn't! Otherwise we'd be dead! We were saved because the hijacker was assured that her child was on her way to Bangkok. Who are you to talk about the danger that is my danger. *(Pause)* And I don't like the way you're looking at me.

NITA: *(Amiable)* The protection of society from dangerous individuals intrigues me. *(Laughs)* Let's see the photos you took.

(Together, they look at photos.)

NITA: Hah! A Thai wedding! The groom is wearing the headdress. And here is a ceremonial mask.

EVELYN: *(Sarcastic)* Like my very own wedding day. When a young woman is about to get married it's usually the happiest time of her life.

NITA: *(Makes a grotesque face causing them both to laugh)* You ought to think of Bush W as a piece of defective wiring.

EVELYN: *(Gleeful)* Yes. Worn out and damaged. *(Pause)* You and I have the flame!

NITA: In Thailand—when you kissed me for the first time, you told me that the soft space above the corner of my lips was...shockingly erotic.

EVELYN: Oh, dearest, dearest, it still is. *(She embraces NITA.)*

NITA: So good that you're home. So good.

EVELYN: Love remembered far away is difficult to trace.

NITA: I remember when I first saw you in tennis clothes. You were so strong and you stood so erect.

EVELYN: Wouldn't it be good to do things just because you wanted to? I don't suppose anyone can ever stay so happy as we were in Thailand.

NITA: Remember Bush and the eyelid incident? That weird night.

EVELYN: Oh yes, I remember that night.

NITA: You had gotten an eyelash in your eye, under the lower lid. You were trying to remove it. I went over to help you and he watched us—then like a stabbed ox he began to bellow and hulk over us!

EVELYN: *(Laughing at NITA's telling of the story)* The lunatic was so suspicious!

NITA: He began to spew out some garbage about a percentage of human females who possess poorly programmed brains! Who became inverts! Inverts! Who fail to reproduce successfully! While I was gently moving your eyelid up and down to dislodge the eyelash, he accused me of trying to blind you! He said that the way I was touching you was perverted! That it made him want to vomit—that it took all his intelligence of spirit to restrain himself from stomping us both to death under his feet—to death and dust under his feet. He said that we reminded him of sick twittering birds looking for a worm in an apple.

EVELYN: Sick twittering birds! *(Laughs)*

NITA: Yes! That's what he said. I don't think it's funny. He's venomous scum!

EVELYN: He is so threatened by you. He thinks death has your face and hands. He tells me that all the time.

NITA: We work wonderfully well together. We break out of ourselves! Concentrating our powers, benefiting each other, taking risks. He says I think like a man. In the oil reclamation business, Evelyn, there are defeats, errors, doubts, brutal realities.

EVELYN: Like the decimation of the elephant. I just know about tennis, and the ancient temples of Thailand, and needlepoint!

NITA: You're fantastic! Fantastic! Earthy! ...Sexy! Woman. Woman!

EVELYN: And what are you?

NITA: I'm just a carcass of evil next to you.

EVELYN: Let me comb your hair. *(She begins combing* NITA's *hair)* The most precious and beautiful hair. It's so lustrous! The miracle of you is unequaled after a thousand years!

NITA: I am part of a long migration of fearless lesbians hardly ever recognized—

EVELYN: Except as the witch in fairytales, concocting potions of flowing menstrual blood, eating young virgins.

NITA: When I told Bush that you wanted to go back to Thailand he said that you constantly try to kill him.

EVELYN: Because of him I've always felt in a state of mourning. He teaches me how to die naked.

NITA: But I don't do that to you.

(They embrace.)

(Scene fades out.)

Scene Five

(Inside the trailer. Low sounds of sludge being dumped. BUSH *stands, grim-faced.)*

BUSH: Evelyn stole my personal diary from its secret place. It was missing for three days. She had copies made. This morning it was put back in its place. The diary directly links me with dumping hazardous waste and the death of that worker. *(Tremulous)* Well, you've got your boy. Step on a crack break my back. She's trying to bewilder me, to lead me into the woods, to blacken the skies around me. She's a stumbling block. Oh, I see you, my perverted wife, silently smelling me out, your jowls and neck in shadow, your vicious eyes of condemnation. I see you leaning over, extending your big leg out, your long fingers scratching and scuttling through the pages. And so you try to satisfy your taste for morbidity at my expense—with my blunders, my confusion. To concoct a massive elaborate fraud! You want me to swallow bile, to dissolve. Death in my house, death outside it. I'm not the only madman with the unthinkable hunger. I will not be her fly-in-a-bottle. I'm strong, resourceful! There are winners and losers. You will know the dimensions of my wrath, criminal woman! I want to be his model and live with his great name for I am this man's son and I'll never bear shame. I'm bitter...furious! Step on a crack break her back!

(Black-out)

Scene Six

(A room in a house. EVELYN *works on her needlepoint.* NITA *watches.)*

EVELYN: Don't stand behind me—sit across from me. I don't like to feel only a presence. I want to see you.

NITA: But you're working on your needlepoint.

EVELYN: I do look up every now and then.

NITA: *(She sits.)* Like this?

EVELYN: *(Admiring the needlepoint)* Nobility of design merits this wonderful silk! The colors and shapes remind me of a fruit, a rock, or a snowflake. *(Pause)* Now, tell me something pleasant. Try to hold still for a few seconds—I want to study the angle of your body. Human figures in needlepoint are difficult to make, you know. *(Inspecting a color)* Hmm, is this aqua or more of a teal blue?

NITA: Something pleasant. Well, the mocking bird can imitate the calls of two hundred different birds, and a cat.

EVELYN: That is cheerful.

NITA: What about something unpleasant?

EVELYN: *(Sighs)* No, thank you. Coming from you, I can guarantee it will be something morbid—like maggots and worms.

NITA: No. Not maggots and worms. A crowd of people on a rock, the flood waters coming up around them.

EVELYN: Do we know the people on that rock?

NITA: We're both on that rock. We could drown.

EVELYN: At least we won't break our necks.

NITA: I could smash it, you know, the maggot.

EVELYN: Hold still, I'm doing an elbow.

NITA: He said that you told him that I stole his personal diary linking him to criminal ventures!

EVELYN: *(Sighs)* I didn't. *(Pause)* I like your new hairstyle, it's so soft and flattering.

NITA: His personal diary filled with dirty little secrets!

EVELYN: Look, dear. The man has a lot of responsibility—a lot of stress. However frail his integrity might appear, it should not be subjected to repeated assaults. I'll give you a little bit of advice, dear. Take him with a grain of salt.

NITA: Since when! I never heard you say that!

EVELYN: You're flapping too much. Be still, dear. I'm working on your elbow. *(Pause)* Years ago, when we were first married, we camped out in the woods one cool summer night. We made love around the glowing embers of the campfire...it crackled and hissed softly like the memory of the day just past. All around us was the silence. Soon we drifted off to sleep, but not before one final look at that incredible star-lit sky which stretched out endlessly like life itself. The next day we drove towards a long steep hill, at the bottom was virgin forest, it circled around us, a pure sapphire light of trees and sun. A breath, a glance could darken or inflame. He wasn't the one who wanted to be there. I wanted to. I loved it. The area was filled with copperheads. We wore high boots and long thick gloves. I felt so courageous. *(Pause)* I took out a gun and fired away at the snakes, the agony of the creatures floated around us. My boot tops were covered with broken pieces of flesh. Suddenly, I turned to Bush and I noticed that one of his eyes was filled with blood. A blood-vessel in his eye had ruptured. He took the gun from my twitching hand. He whispered just one word several times, "why, why?", he said. He was the one with compassion—not me. Nita, there is the vastness...the smallness...of the forest. And the ruthless and cold-blooded. *(Instructive)* Nita, if you feel remorse or regret about something that you do or did—remember that you have certain privileges, and you can't escape them. *(Laughs)* But then why should you want to?

NITA: Because I must. Catastrophe waits.

EVELYN: Catastrophe waits! Melodramatic, dear? Foretelling disasters are probably not much fun. They're your own bizarre perceptions. You have bad nerves, dear. *(Pause)* You wished that the hijacker had blown up the plane—the plane that I was on.

NITA: *(Angry)* He was the one who said it! Not me!

EVELYN: You even had the gall to destroy important research information on environmental danger. Information concerning exposure to pollutants and toxic agents.

NITA: He told you that?

EVELYN: No.

NITA: Well, then who?!

EVELYN: I can't tell you because I don't know who it was. It was just a voice on the telephone.

NITA: A voice on the telephone. Did you tell Bush?

EVELYN: I did.

NITA: What did he say?

EVELYN: That he would discuss the matter with you. *(Pause)* Hand me some pins, dear.

NITA: Get them yourself!

EVELYN: Now, that's an inhuman snarl. Not a response. *(Laughs)* They're in that little box.

NITA: *(Flinging the box next to her. She picks up the ring case that fell out of the box.)* What's this? For me?

EVELYN: *(Begrudgingly)* Now, who else might it be for—a thieving Gypsy with one eye?

NITA: A sapphire! It's beautiful!

EVELYN: It was my mother's. She would not have approved of my giving it to you. There's a head-on fiery battle. What can I do? I need you. *(Embracing NITA)* In a poor land, I longed for you, for want of your fair hand. Everything is beginning for you. For me the hour is always the same. *(Laughs)* Now, I'm thinking of elephants! There were elephants in Thailand. Now, they're an endangered species.

NITA: I know.

EVELYN: Of course, you know. Actually, it's one particular elephant that I'm thinking of. Did I ever tell you this story?

NITA: *(Gently)* Yes, you have.

EVELYN: Years ago, in Thailand, Bush and I stayed at a hotel that was as large and grand as a palace. In the courtyard was an elephant. I could see it from my bedroom window. I loved its simplicity and naturalness. In the morning I would call out, "hello there", and at bedtime, "goodnight". One afternoon, I went down into the courtyard, I stood only about two feet away from it. The calm motion of its sway was soothing and peaceful to my being.

We gazed serenely at each other. The creature's eyes were fringed with enormously long eyelashes. We shared a profound emotion, mysterious and marvelous. The elephant swayed from side to side as in a dance, and I began to sway, too. Suddenly, the great trunk roped out towards me and instinctively I jumped backwards out of its urgent reach—and ran away. *(Pause)* Later, when I told Bush, he just snickered and said that I should have let myself be swept off my feet by the elephant—and that the lack was in me because I had not shown trust.

(Black-out)

Scene Seven

(BUSH stands in front of a lectern. He wears a black academic cap and gown. His tone is respectable and properly humble.)

BUSH: I am deeply moved to have you bestow upon me this honorary doctor's degree, thus finding me worthy of the highest recognition a man of this world can receive, that of his Alma Mater. There are always people in this world who prove humanity's heart by extraordinary strength and perseverance when neither seems possible. And so I urge you not to disparage the humanities, total dependence on science does little to aid the search for personal and spiritual fulfillment, which is the real business of living. To help young people with their education and give encouragement, to pay tribute to those who are outstanding in the community, to fill one's life with good works, to be an inspiration to all as everybody's image of the good neighbor, and most of all, to give gifts of charity anonymously. Virtues are habits which confer upon man a skill in acting well. *(His gestures and tone are grandiose and tyrannical:)* I am the unseen donor who gives ridicule, the striking poison that rots your bones! That scourges your heart! Your struggle against me is futile! Know that I live and murder! Sup on my lethal mixtures, my toxic pestilence! I'm getting rich and richer! Squeeze my righteousness hard! Rest your head on a great stone! Stone your head on a great stone! Go to a great stone and rest your head! Who can know what I can do! The one I'm against is you! And so I cast my fate with myself!

(Low sound of sludge)

(Lights fade to blackness.)

Scene Eight

(Inside the trailer. NITA is standing near a child's bicycle. After a moment, BUSH enters.)

BUSH: Whose bicycle?

NITA: It's a present for Pete's daughter. I bought it because the human and the natural are as much a part of us as blood and guilt.

BUSH: Indeed. But where are the foxtails? The bicycle that I owned as a boy had a foxtail attached to the seat. When I raced along—that foxtail shot straight out behind me! What did you buy for Pete's crippled boy?

NITA: A picture puzzle.

BUSH: *(Leafing through folder)* Well, what's the picture of?

NITA: A boy playing with his dog.

BUSH: Wonderful. There is something about a dog that gets you. The eyes of a dog, the expression of a dog, the wagging tail of a dog, and the cold damp nose of a dog are all God-given for one purpose only to make complete fools of us human beings.

NITA: Pete said that there will be an investigation of a corruption scandal about illegal dumping of toxic waste.

BUSH: *(Ignoring her)* And my bitch Evelyn prevented me from owning a dog because of her asthma. Spiteful woman. May dachshunds eat her!

NITA: Do you trust Pete?

BUSH: Like my own hands. He's a good family man. A man like Pete is the backbone of this nation.

NITA: He made a pass at me.

BUSH: Oh, he did, did he? What did he do? Did he whistle at ya?

NITA: He ogled me.

BUSH: Ogled you? I thought, maybe, he diddled you. You know, when he first saw you he asked if you were 'the wife". He didn't say, is she your wife? He said, "Is she the wife?"

NITA: What did you say?

BUSH: That you weren't the wife. He said that you looked like a hot piece.

NITA: That was disrespectful of him. Did you chastise him?

BUSH: No. *(Pause)* When you first came to America, Evelyn told me that you had been a prostitute in Thailand.

NITA: Tell me, if you had been a woman, wouldn't you have liked being a prostitute?

BUSH: No, I wouldn't. Not with my patrician background.

NITA: Perhaps, if you were starving—

BUSH: Starvation would never occur to me. Nita, sometimes you think like a beggar. *(Lewdly)* You have the dirtiest mouth of any woman that I've ever seen. Roses whose haunting beauty echoes thy lips.

(He embraces her. She doesn't respond. He gently pushes her away.)

NITA: The hotel reservations from Salzburg came.

BUSH: Good. Summer is always pleasant in Salzburg. I've made arrangements for the three of us to be there at festival time. We'll stay at the same small elegant hotel that my parents visited when they were newlyweds, The Silver Stag.

(Lights fade to blackness.)

Scene Nine

(In Salzburg. EVELYN and BUSH are having tea in the lounge. The mood is friendly and open.)

EVELYN: As a little girl in Thailand, Nita gathered summer flowers for the Buddhist monks. There was one that she hated and so for spite she hid a chicken head in a bouquet and gave it to her hateful monk. Naturally, it didn't bother him. He simply said, "I see it all! I see everything!" *(Laughs)*

BUSH: A wonderful story!

EVELYN: *(Sighs)* The monk's reaction made her numb...cold...distorted. What does she want?

BUSH: To work hard, to have fun. Often, my most difficult task is explaining to my employees what they might be doing wrong and might be doing better. It is a challenge.

EVELYN: You do succeed, though.

BUSH: I try to find rational solutions to dilemmas. You have a powerful impact on Nita. You enjoy that, don't you?

EVELYN: *(Tremulous)* I don't want to...darling.

BUSH: *(Gently taking her hand)* Oh, my dearest...

EVELYN: *(Moved)* We can avoid the worst consequence if we cooperate... but will we?

BUSH: Oh, my dearest, my dearest...

EVELYN: I'm pessimistic about Nita's marrying someone. I want her to marry and have children. There is such warmth and gentleness to children. She must marry someone.

BUSH: Whether she chooses to marry someone or not to marry someone is beyond our control. You know that, dearest.

EVELYN: I don't want us to be the reason for her not marrying someone.

BUSH: She never criticizes you, dearest.

EVELYN: No, not audaciously at least.

BUSH: What a woman you are. Is there one of us who cannot plead guilty to having indulged Nita?

EVELYN: Oh, I know. She's a champion at heart-stealing.

BUSH: Her mind very willingly enjoys as many indulgences as it can persuade us to offer. Her brain is never slow to take advantage of us.

EVELYN: (Reflective) Everytime I'd open a door she was behind it. I should flay the life out of her. I won't know what to do if she doesn't marry someone.

BUSH: I understand, my dearest. What is apparent, though, is that despite her independence she needs to be protected.

EVELYN: She's my treasure.

BUSH: And so be it. She's true-blue. A generous girl.

EVELYN: Yes, she's forever giving and making others happy. (Poetic) 'Tis the season to enjoy picked berries, music, and sweet girls...

BUSH: You know, you both are alluring women. It's a matter of your touch, seductive women have the right touch. You snuggle in so close to a human heart.

EVELYN: (Intense) She is my sole source. To feel her is to feel a snarl of honeysuckle. Sometimes, to annoy me, she would tap her foot incessantly. I would grab her knee under the table, holding her leg down, and ask her not to do it.

BUSH: We're feeling pretty good about ourselves. And why not? Here, in Salzburg, my energy and ambition return in full force!

(NITA enters. BUSH and EVELYN adroitly change the subject.)

BUSH: Pete's burden is heavy, indeed—that crippled son.

EVELYN: But you've helped relieve some of the burden!

BUSH: Well, I gave him some excellent investment advice.

EVELYN: You did what you could. That's all one can do in life.

BUSH: Pete's my rock.

EVELYN: Well, that's something precious, reliability.

BUSH: He knows how to run the store.

EVELYN: I wonder if either of you realize that by the end of the century households will be comprised of people who are related by neither blood nor marriage.

NITA: Really.

BUSH: *(Indignant)* Evelyn means that the business of survival must be shared.

EVELYN: That's right, dear. Young people aren't marrying as often as they used to. My brother lived with a girl for ten years, he met her when he was twenty years old—in Alaska!

BUSH: What type of people go to Alaska?

EVELYN: All kinds of people.

NITA: Was she attractive?

EVELYN: Little attention is paid to physical appearance in Alaska.

NITA: I didn't ask that!

BUSH: Don't bite her head off!

EVELYN: As a matter of fact she was a pretty girl. In the beginning of the relationship they couldn't be pulled apart.

NITA: What happened, finally.

EVELYN: It ended—that's what happened. He's been floundering ever since.

NITA: Like me. *(Laugh)*

EVELYN: But you have a career. You're lavishly paid!

BUSH: She's right, Nita. If it wasn't for her good head Nita would be a cork bobbing up and down in a sea of uncertainty and change!

EVELYN: *(Laughs)* Now, Bush, stop that. *(Indicating NITA)* This one can be very defiant! She left kith and kin in Thailand! I never would have left family!

BUSH: She's a damn hard worker.

EVELYN: Yes! And she's neglecting herself!

BUSH: Financially independent!

EVELYN: That's beside the point! Just take a look at her skin—her mouth—how red and irritated! Wonderful cosmetologists all over Salzburg—and she won't take advantage!

NITA: I'm alright.

BUSH: No, oh, no. You look worn down. Stay home—rest tonight.

EVELYN: Well, I'm staying in tonight. You two can dine together.

BUSH: Are you not up to par, dear?

EVELYN: A little tired. I'll rest tonight—do some of my needlepoint.

BUSH: Evelyn, I want us to enjoy the festivities. I want us to stand together on the terrace overlooking the square. We could hear the music!

EVELYN: What do you want to do, Nita?

BUSH: Nita wants to stay in her pretty little room.

NITA: I feel like shampooing tonight.

EVELYN: Go out to dinner with him.

BUSH: *(Laughs)* I should wash my hands of you both! Evenlyn, let's go to the fair, please dear.

EVELYN: Nita, your hair looks fine. Don't bother shampooing tonight—it's too chilly.

BUSH: *(To NITA)* There are those documents to check—the reports that Pete gave you, remember? I want them later this evening.

(Lights fade to blackness.)

Scene Ten

(In Salzburg. BUSH and TANYA are together. Her make-up is eerie. The mood is ominous.)

TANYA: I imagine you differently than you are. That's dishonest? No. Honesty is as good as dead flowers.

BUSH: I want you.

TANYA: Hooray for Tanya. What else?

BUSH: To be where nothing is wasted and nothing is spoiled.

TANYA: Philosophy!

BUSH: No, just my ideas, a synthesis of the past and future. *(Pause)* Things that make a man unique make it necessary that he be cared for—truly cared for. As I assess the last two precarious years, gain and loss, how shall I think of myself and what I am, that which formed me, made me unique?

TANYA: Every man is different in the beginning. Why do men pay more for Tanya when another whore is every bit as good?

BUSH: You tell me.

TANYA: Because I'm a whore that gives a lot of taste without a lot of work. I'm a valve, I can be turned on.

BUSH: Oh, I like that. And then?

TANYA: I sneak a hot bath whenever I get an hour to myself. *(Pause)* In my backyard was an old apple tree, its branches had grown thick and tangled, its fruit was mean fruit, shriveled and sour. Last winter I gave it a hard pruning, so hard I was afraid I'd killed it. But this spring it branched and flowered, expanding towards the sun.

BUSH: Hooray for Tanya.

TANYA: Dark moods pass, you see. When my mother abandoned my father I was eleven.

BUSH: Where is she now, Tanya?

TANYA: In South America. She escaped to a spiritual life and married a preacher.

BUSH: Does she write to you?

TANYA: No. But he does. He sends me religious books. She has money. I'll inherit her money.

BUSH: Will you see her?

TANYA: I don't know. If I do...I will vomit on her hands...only to make it bearable. You see...I'm curious about her, that's all. I could use the money.

BUSH: She might not leave you any.

TANYA: Well, that's true. Yes. I can see her side...why she left. That's my dilemma. I'm divided between love and hate...the direction goes towards hate...the first killing frost. What do you think of that?

BUSH: I can't imagine what's in your head. Do you remember her?

TANYA: Yes, especially her legs. We played a game. She'd hoist me up with her feet! She'd lie on her back, brace her feet against my thighs and fly me through the air! I loved it! And the light scattering around her hair.

BUSH: *(He embraces her.)* You're a little cracked. I like that. I bet that you can cause more trouble than the Mediterranean fruit fly.

TANYA: The force and purity of my nature. Is your wife in Salzburg?

BUSH: Yes.

TANYA: Is she dying?

BUSH: No.

TANYA: Some men say that their wives are dying. It explains their plight of why they go to a prostitute. *(Pause)* Your wife is here in Salzburg?

BUSH: I've told you—yes. And we do make love.

TANYA: Do you quiver when you do it?

BUSH: *(Ignoring her)* How often do you work, Tanya?

TANYA: Three or four days a week. Not during the day, late afternoon and evenings, most of the time. You have me for the whole week. The best comes last for you.

BUSH: I'm a lucky fellow. What will you do mornings?

TANYA: I'll work out in the gym. I'm fat here and there.

BUSH: Your fertile belly...is lovely.

TANYA: Inside, it's like corrugated cardboard.

(BUSH *staggers.*)

TANYA: What's wrong with you?

BUSH: I have a weak blood vessel in my eye. A war injury.

TANYA: You look strong and healthy.

BUSH: *(Pounding his waist)* Feel that! It's hard!

TANYA: Your fertile belly.

BUSH: *(Embracing her)* I'm a lonely man, Tanya.

TANYA: It's a mystery that you're attracted to me. Your type usually isn't.

BUSH: Why? You're very lovely.

TANYA: Only to farmers, shepherds, traveling musicians, acrobats and florists.

BUSH: Florists?

TANYA: I can never pass by a flower shop without wanting to seduce the florist. Pots of radiant blossoms bid welcome.

BUSH: How whimsical of you.

TANYA: I know my body well. *(Pause)* You're a sad man.

BUSH: Why do you say that to me?

TANYA: Your wife is harming you. You know that.

BUSH: She's ill. I'm very lonely. *(Pause)* There aren't any children at home. I'm a father to my employees. I love them. They provide the continuity to my life. I wanted a close union only with my wife. I want peace... contentment. She won't change...her weaknesses. I must defend my well-being. A man must. Right!

TANYA: *(Amused)* You like to have sex in strange cities. You are gentle... violent. I know how to stimulate you...all you need is one beautiful urge. I am the kind of woman who wants you. *(Pause)* I don't care about children. I don't like them. It's disastrous to bring children into the world.

(Lights fade to blackness. End of ACT ONE)

ACT TWO

Scene Eleven

(A room in a house. EVELYN and NITA are together. A radio plays, softly.)

NITA: We would try to mist the plants several times in the morning when the sun streamed in the windows.

(Suddenly, there is a loud banging at the door.)

EVELYN: It's open!

BUSH: *(He storms in.)* Are you staying in this evening, Nita?

NITA: I'm going with you both to the opera!

BUSH: What do you think of staying in tonight, Nita!

NITA: The original plan was for us to be together this evening.

BUSH: I have a new fresh idea! You're staying in all by your lonesome! Turn the radio off!

(NITA stares at him and EVELYN looks away.)

BUSH: You will turn the radio off!

(BUSH lunges at NITA and starts to drag her across the floor. NITA struggles and EVELYN picks up a figurine and menaces BUSH. They glare at each other, he releases NITA and stands looking at the women, he is shaking with rage.)

EVELYN: Get out!

(BUSH exits.)

EVELYN: He hurt you! He hurt you! That scum! Divide and conquer!

NITA: Yes, like Caesar!

EVELYN: There was no justification! No justification!

NITA: There never is.

EVELYN: What poison is sliding around in his mind?

NITA: He's making us go on a death march! I want you to leave him, Evelyn. I want you to come with me.

EVELYN: He had no right to crash in like that! No right!

NITA: Leave him!

EVELYN: What's wrong with him? He's so envious!

NITA: He's the walking dead! You're not going to win.

EVELYN: I thought he was enjoying himself with Tanya—

NITA: Enjoying himself! He rots a little more each day.

EVELYN: There's nothing I can do. Bear with us! Bear with us! He works more than ten hours a day running the business!

NITA: You're so useless, Evelyn.

EVELYN: Will that be in my obituary? That I was a useless woman?

NITA: Your needlepoint work...your tennis playing...your scholarly research on Asia...it's all useless, like you. (*Pause*) How much money do you earn, Evelyn? When I was in prison, on a false charge, I learned a trade. You're right, he works hard—so do I!

EVELYN: Understanding and more sympathy, that's what he needs. (*Pause*) Patience, patience...we have inside us golden Sunday mornings—

NITA: Tell me another story.

EVELYN: Warmth...devotion...sweet rituals.

NITA: Sweet rituals! They sound soggy!

EVELYN: I'm not a useless woman.

NITA: You're a goldfish swimming around—

EVELYN: Be quiet! You will not orchestrate our lives! In spite of you I will retain my link to the world!

NITA: Your link to the world!

EVELYN: Yes! For you to want and seek admission means nothing—you're never at ease in the world! You don't have the credentials! It would be nicer without you...but whoever is here is here. (*Pause*) Sometimes, when I felt the need of a girl's body, I would concentrate on an image, a scene from a tapestry, and then the desire stopped. I felt in perfect harmony, quite contemplative. I'm just a traveler, really, a lover of the picturesque—

NITA: And the bizarre!

EVELYN: I always knew that I would meet you in a palace or in a cave. Everything is miraculous in my world. I don't want to mangle anything. Nita, don't wish our destruction. (*Pause*) There was once a traveler who lost her way in the woods. The darkness made her afraid. Terror was everywhere. Suddenly, a storm broke and the lightning illuminated the road before her. She found her way back to the world. (*Pause*) You know, Tanya really is a valuable whore.

NITA: An enticing whore. She did all the things he hoped she would. An infidelity made in heaven.

EVELYN: It's true.

NITA: What did she wear? What was her face like? Her hair? Her body? Was she an exquisite sensual bitch?

EVELYN: She was the whole female world.

NITA: Did you actually see her? Tanya?

EVELYN: Yes, I saw her.

NITA: What was her face like?

EVELYN: Proud, strong. She wore a black lace dress, and a twisted coal-black bead choker with bright blue beads. *(Pause)* Keep in mind, that he's highly respected! Highly respected as a man firmly in control of the company's destiny.

NITA: I'm well aware of it!

EVELYN: His reputation must never be sullied.

NITA: If it is—I could take over. I'm his successor.

EVELYN: You must not raise your hopes too high, dear.

NITA: No, I might be in for a disappointment.

EVELYN: *(Intense)* Do you know that the whore is very particular from her lips to fingertips? The kind that demands constant devotion.

NITA: And surprises lurk around every corner. *(She exits.)*

EVELYN: *(Angry)* Where are you going? Why don't you answer?

(The door bangs shut.)

EVELYN: She dares to bang my door! I haven't any comfort with that one! *(Pause)* The night he was with Tanya, after dessert, when coffee was served. Bush reached inside his jacket and withdrew a cigar. The whore reached across the table and took it from him. He smiled, she bit off the end of the cigar with slightly parted lips, exposing white teeth. Then she moistened it with the tip of her tongue, and slowly lit it. She threw back her head and blew smoke toward the ceiling. Then she leaned across the table to say something to him. She held the cigar in her strong fingers, off to the side of her face, oblivious to everything except the man. Every so often she would hand the cigar across the table, and the man would puff on it for awhile before handing it back to her—

NITA: *(Enters)* He had a binge with a whore! And you're getting turned on—by his binge with a whore!

EVELYN: You dirty little monkey! What would you know about it?! It's odd how you make enemies wherever you go. He warned me that you'd become a problem.

NITA: I don't want to argue—

EVELYN: Your bad nerves! Your bad nerves! I was the one who found you—who brought you to America! I was the one who made him accept you! I hope I survive the mistakes of the past!

NITA: When you brought me to America, I was wearing a white cotton dirndl that you had made. *(Pause)* You always gave special care...to me. *(Restraining tears)* In the evening, you would read books to me. I remember the small hotel on top of a mountain where we spent a night. We watched the sunrise with the sun shining on the mountain top while the country down below was still in darkness.

EVELYN: *(Reflective)* I remember that white dirndl that I made for you. It had lace...lace is so inviting to the touch...the texture of rounded edges so pleasing. Fifty years ago, society ladies displayed their collections on gold-edged boards. A popular tea-time diversion. Tanya wore black lace. Her skin is luminous...even the jasmine flowers became dull compared to her skin. Nita, wouldn't you like to be alone with her and take all her clothes off? The soul is nourished by the purity of childlike beauty. You'd like to photograph Tanya, wouldn't you? You'd have as much control over yourself as a moth flying around a candle. As long as you kept a camera in your hands, you'd be safe. Tanya is every red-blooded man's dream. Where is Bush? Did you see him? You said vicious things to him! Why?!

NITA: He asked me to. *(Laughs)*

EVELYN: You have an ugly heart.

NITA: But it was night time and he couldn't see the look on my face.

EVELYN: That wet look of yours! He was ready for you! *(Pause)* Tucked away in a far corner of his brain lie the soft and tender feelings. I wish he wouldn't deny them. *(Pause)* Hotel, sunrise...I don't remember a hotel. This place is not what I expected. The guests are remote...I stand in horror of the food...mainly, it's the guests—

NITA: Perhaps, we committed some social blunder.

EVELYN: *(Salacious)* I can't think of any, sweetie. I never fondle you in the dining room. Wind-swept deserts and gypsy caravans, that's what Tanya brings to mind. She'd look delicious in white. I want to take Tanya and Bush for a day of swimming in the countryside outside Salzburg.

NITA: A day of swimming—are you going to stick her in the mud or him?

EVELYN: Nita, being kind isn't really so hard if only you would try. You disappoint me. Bush complains of headaches and nausea. The countryside will do him good.

NITA: And us?

EVELYN: I've been very tolerant with you. I've enabled you to devote time and attention to your career—more than you deserve. I wanted Salzburg to be a time of love and trust between us. You disappoint me. When I meet Tanya, I'm going to say five little words...hello, hello, my darling girl. She'll come to me. We'll watch the trees breathe. I'll hand her an orange...she'll eat it pulp and rind. We'll let desire run into our bodies. She will not be a cold girl. She will not want to miss out on any of my stories.

NITA: *(She picks up a folder and leafs through it.)* Your message to me is clear. I don't have the correct qualifications. I'm not accessible or elusive like Tanya. You'll just have to bear with me.

EVELYN: What do you really do?!

NITA: I get up in the morning. I go to work.

EVELYN: My husband and I have reason to believe that you're destructive!

NITA: Remember, I am a displaced person.

EVELYN: Well, then tell me—what does it feel like to be a displaced person? Do you feel you have been deprived of seeing the world whole, and want revenge? You've given us good reason to fear you. You attempted to use the state police to confiscate business records!

NITA: Soon, we'll leave Salzburg. We'll be home. You'll be able to read your books once again and do your needlepoint...your most accomplished art.

(Lights fade to blackness.)

Scene Twelve

(Visual image of EVELYN placing a necklace around NITA's neck. A room in a house. The music of Chopin is playing, softly. EVELYN sits on the settee. BUSH enters and watches her a long while. She is not aware of his presence. He is in black-tie.)

BUSH: You've granted me a considerable service, Evelyn, dear.

EVELYN: *(Stammers)* D-d-d-d-dining with Tanya? I don't mind.

BUSH: *(Patronizing)* My needs slide down your throat as easily as custard.

EVELYN: You'll describe in detail Tanya's gown, her shoes?

BUSH: Yes, dear. All the lush colors and intricacy of her beauteous form. *(He pours two glasses of wine and hands her a glass.)* Here in Salzburg, *gemutlich* says it all—good-natured, cozy, comfortable.

EVELYN: We'll relax because the air is good.

BUSH: These mountains!

EVELYN: The rich and the beautiful flock to Salzburg to see and be seen. They play like children on holiday.

BUSH: Holidays are for the child in all of us, dear.

EVELYN: *(Reflective)* The eyes of a rich man twinkle with life. His smile casts a warm glow, his gentleness is a reminder of care. And those who have seen Bush play, see joy.

BUSH: *(He approaches her and kisses her on the neck.)* And the rewards and perils of my rich bitch.

EVELYN: Kiss me on the mouth.

(BUSH turns his back on her.)

EVELYN: It's pretty, that necklace that Nita wore this afternoon.

BUSH: It is pretty, dear.

EVELYN: She has a lover.

BUSH: *(Ironic)* Who might it be, dear—someone with a stain on his character?

EVELYN: I'm afraid so. *(Stammers)* He-he-he-he-he-he's a thief—a forger!

BUSH: The toads are tumbling out of your mouth, dear.

EVELYN: She wants to marry him!

BUSH: Tell me about him, dear.

EVELYN: I'm afraid he's scum. She attracts scum. She always has. Stop looking at me that way!

BUSH: Now, now, Evelyn. You surprise me.

EVELYN: They have nothing in common! He preys on her! Their lives and their personalities are vastly different. He worked in a copper mine.

BUSH: *(Jovial)* He shan't make her a proper husband?

EVELYN: No. He'll ruin my girl.

BUSH: Have you two had it out?

EVELYN: She won't listen. The day she listens—I'll be an old woman dusting my needlepoint!

BUSH: What does he look like? The scum.

EVELYN: He's a big man. He drives a big Lincoln with a car phone. In college he was a big foot-ball star. He wants single-handedly to run everything.

BUSH: Well, if Nita is in love, so be it! Perhaps, the man will make her happy. You do want her to marry someone.

EVELYN: Not that one. She should have married my brother. He wanted to marry her!

BUSH: Now, now, dear.

EVELYN: I don't want her to throw herself away, you know.

BUSH: Let her love the journey of life.

EVELYN: *(She picks up her needle-point and shows it to him. He barely looks at it.)* She rips up my needlepoint. I don't know why. Years ago, she cut my belt in half. It was navy-blue leather. She said she needed a belt. She took it without asking permission. I found it later. She had cut a piece off and punctured a hole into it so it would fit around her small waist. I'm too, too generous with her. She takes me for granted. I was the one who brought her from Thailand. She was adorable.

BUSH: Now, she's a bit scrawny in the shank.

EVELYN: She is not. She has lovely legs.

BUSH: *(Coldly)* You're the one with the legs.

EVELYN: I have broken veins, blue spidery blotches near my knees...a few scars because of that fire. Do you remember?

BUSH: No. I was at sea.

EVELYN: In the hospital, Nita would sing to me...her moist oval lips like a Christmas caroler in the snow. Why couldn't I fall into her arms without falling into her hands? What happened?

BUSH: *(Jovial)* You got burned.

EVELYN: She would sit with me for hours, with her hands resting on her knees, attentive...sensitive. I did love her then.

BUSH: Who loves the most, dear?

(Blackout)

Scene Thirteen

(In the hotel lounge. NITA is looking out of a window, watching EVELYN play tennis. BUSH sits facing the audience.)

BUSH: Does my wife Evelyn look fit?

NITA: Superbly fit.

BUSH: How does she look?

NITA: Get up and see for yourself.

BUSH: *(He goes to the window, limping slightly.)* Her skin glows! The challenge of the game makes her skin glow! No matter what her age—she'll have that skin! Mastering a physical skill can boost mind and body.

NITA: *(Amused)* Life is too short and winter too long to go without mink.

BUSH: What's that?

NITA: I was just thinking of the photo I took of Evelyn. She was nude except for a white mink coat draped around her shoulders, fur against her skin. She was standing with her back towards the camera, her rump gleamed in the moonlight.

BUSH: Her what?

NITA: Her rump!

BUSH: Oh, yes. I remember the photo. Evelyn my wife certainly knows how to enjoy herself. Body and soul. She loves to dance.

(BUSH *tries to dance with* NITA. *She moves away from him.*)

BUSH: Well, you can't have too many fond memories.

(Jazz softly plays. NITA *strikes seductive poses.* BUSH *watches.* EVELYN *enters. She is unaware of them.)*

EVELYN: My mind drifts in and out, abandoned to dreams, legends, mysterious divinities. Remembrances of silken touches, sunlight warm on her breasts, the lacy butterfly at her bodice, quite a bit of gorgeous ass. Temptation abounds. The color, subtle twilight lavender, come close, touch it, touch it.

(EVELYN and NITA *move towards each other and begin to dance.* BUSH *sits in the shadows. The following sequences are juxtaposed.)*

EVELYN: Since our wedding day, our surroundings were equally important to us. Remember, dear? The trees, the gardens, the pool. We've always been passionate about style.

(Lights up on BUSH. EVELYN *and* NITA *freeze as he speaks.)*

BUSH: I love getting the bones deformed!

EVELYN: When we were first married, we redid the cornices of the house and all of the windows. I loved covering the walls with a melon-toned stapled wallpaper. The floor came from a barn. A practical way of dealing with incoming dogs and wet boots.

BUSH: They suffer from pains in the head! They cough up blood! Brain tumors the size of lemons! I must confess that when I contemplate damaged bodies—O noble death rays!

EVELYN: I must say that I liked the mixture of Italian marble and white formica. Eclectic! False windows with Gothic tops, more elegance. A Chinese Chippendale porch trellis.

BUSH: An unmistaken inhuman way of dying!

EVELYN: Lovely, soft warm colors, a cloud of dried baby's breath, an English medallion chair 1770, freshened with white paint. I've always been passionate about beautiful architecture, interiors, superb taste and judgment.

BUSH: Brain tumors the size of lemons!

EVELYN: We cooked our favorite meals.

(NITA *exits.*)

(*Black-out*)

(*Lights up*)

BUSH: (*Bitter*) I hate autumn...the first chill. My skin hurts.

EVELYN: Well, let's make a fire.

BUSH: I don't want to sit in front of a crackling fire, looking out of windows.

EVELYN: Oh, I love the rust and gold of the trees. Don't you?

BUSH: I'm cold.

EVELYN: I'll knit you a beautiful warm sweater.

BUSH: My legs are cold.

EVELYN: I'll tuck a patchwork quilt around you. We'll drink steaming mugs of hot buttered rum.

BUSH: (*Sarcastic*) Now what could be more cozy than that?!

EVELYN: What's wrong?

BUSH: You don't like autumn anymore than I do. (*Pause*) Well, why don't you answer?! Has the cat got your tongue?

EVELYN: No.

BUSH: Well, you just watch out then. (*Pause*) Do you think I should continue seeing Tanya? Nita thinks that Tanya is doing me a world of good.

EVELYN: (*She goes to him, placing her hands on his shoulders.*) Bush, that's not you.

BUSH: She gives the come-on to Pete. Can you imagine? —With one of my truckers! She's a damn fool! You should tell her to stop.

EVELYN: I promise. *(Pause)* What time is it?

BUSH: It's three A M. Can't you sleep?

EVELYN: No. I can't sleep. *(She starts to exit.)* I'll scrub the bathtub.

BUSH: *(Gentle)* You do these menial things...even now. You shouldn't have to do them.

EVELYN: I want to do it. *(She exits.)*

BUSH: You should pile your hair atop your head so that it falls in beguiling tendrils around the nape of your sweet neck. You look so wan, so tragic. Here, let me help you slip into the silk kimono that I bought for you, Evelyn. *(Sings)*
Just when you think
That she is your pal
You look for her
And find her
Hanging 'round some
Other gal.

(Lights fade to blackness.)

Scene Fourteen

(A room in a house. EVELYN and NITA are together.)

EVELYN: He wants you to leave. He hasn't told you because I won't let him. You're not going anywhere. *(Pause)* The more you know, the more you'll want to go. He says I should live in our home in the country. If I scream you wouldn't hear things I'll never be able to tell about! I try to cope as best I can. It's true—I did nothing to help myself until you came along. *(Pause)* When he saw what we were, he called us "frenzied cockroaches." I laughed at him. I use the pressure to my advantage. Tanya is too young for him...but not for me. Remember what you said...that I would have been happier marrying a rotten log swarming with white ants.

NITA: You should never have married.

EVELYN: I just didn't see how I wasn't going to marry. Man needs woman...I will always keep extending a hand for one in need. But you and I have accomplished a wonderful feat!

NITA: What feat have we accomplished?

EVELYN: *(Laughs)* We're still close.

NITA: And Bush and Tanya?

EVELYN: I'm sure they're affectionate with each other.

NITA: If you mean that their groins respond to each other's. I'm like you, Evelyn. Sometimes I dream as you instead of myself between the darkness and daylight.

EVELYN: *(Intense)* Tell me what you are.

NITA: I'm a woman whose arteries and veins are made of rusty wire and sticky eggshells.

EVELYN: *(Amused)* What were you when I found you?

NITA: I had been convicted of drug smuggling, burglary, and murder.

EVELYN: And what did you do?

NITA: *(Trance-like)* When my name is called I step forward. I nod to the guard.

EVELYN: What do you say?

NITA: Here—I'm here.

EVELYN: What else do you do?

NITA: I eat the same food that the inmates eat.

EVELYN: And what else?

NITA: I sleep where they sleep. I hold them. *(Pause)* A woman walks by the guards at the iron gate, a prisoner with tattoos from her neck to her waist. She pulls up her skirt and shows me a scar on her abdomen. She asks me if I can get her some medicine. Another prisoner pulls down her lower lip, and requests special bridgework. Another asks me for warm milk. *(Pause)* I calmed them. I'd touch them and listen to them cry. No one is more forgotten than the prisoners. On cool mornings I approach the shivering women. They tell me their names, aliases, and crimes. Some would say that they had never been in jail before.

EVELYN: *(Embracing* NITA*)* There was a little girl who had a little curl right in the middle of her face...and when she was good she was very, very good....

(Lights fade to blackness. Lights slowly come up.)

BUSH: *(Intense)* According to Benjamin Franklin there are only three faithful things! An old wife, an old dog, and ready money! Leave things the way they are? I will not! And giants walked the earth in those days! I have mastery over people and goods! I am a warrior! A chieftain! A mercenary! A sorcerer! Lord of battle! Street commando! Gangster-daddy! Doc Holiday! Lord of the outlaw kings! Hardcore professional career criminal! I was pulled, dragged by a ring in my nose, like a lamb in a god-forsaken field of snow! But today—Tanya! Tanya! Her mystery, her charisma! Oh, how I am ripe for her love! The two of us on an unforgettable holiday in this centuries old European city. Culture and tradition! Evelyn was born in Ketchum, Idaho! Hah! *(Twang)* I'll take little old you to a big old brew! Last night,

Tanya and I swam in the heated outdoor swimming pool. She's a stunning piece! Then a gourmet dinner by candlelight. I will buy my stunning piece splendid finery—poison—each generation passes along to the next—cherish it—poison! Evelyn has hundreds of lips and eyes! She frightens me—where dreams come true—at the foot of her grave I'll stand—my legs wide apart! Witch-face! Witch-face! The head of the woman horrifies me—haunts—refuses! Her nose is deformed, her mouth, broad and grimacing! Boar tusks protrude from her cheeks, mud and plant fibers leak from her nipples! Faces and forms of demons! Devil! Clown! Woman! Spook! Spook! Stop mocking me! Tanya had a grimace! No! No! Evelyn grimaces! Tanya is beautiful, splendid! Tanya's skin is taut, smoothed to perfection! Healthy! Woman, matron, model of proper behavior. Tawdry slut! Buffoons that make me laugh! Ugly! I will buy my stunning piece jewels for her gleaming satin skin! Then cherish it! Then cherish it! Evelyn harasses me! She is like a sack of hate that stretches, shifts and changes shape! Mask! Fetish! Cult figure! Volcanic rock cunt! *(He writhes, clutching his head and falls.)*

(Black-out. The lights slowly come up. The stage is bathed in a bluish glow. EVELYN *and* NITA *are sitting together. The mood is peaceful. Lights dim out.)*

Scene Fifteen

(Inside the trailer. NITA *is sitting at the desk.* BUSH *is sitting in the shadows. The telephone rings.)*

NITA: *(Answering)* Yes, Pete. *(Pause)* Oh, I'm so glad that your little girl likes the bicycle. And your son is working on the puzzle. Good. *(Pause)* You're very welcome, Pete. *(Pause)* Yes, there is a possibility that later in the year Mr W will retire and live in Europe for awhile. *(Pause)* It's not a serious illness. Mr W has a strong constitution. *(Pause)* Well, he suffers disorders of taste and smell. *(Pause)* It's business as usual around here. No problem. *(Firm)* Be on time! Midnight! *(She hangs up phone, and looks over papers.)* I want to have the right rapport with Pete. It makes things easier. He knows about the death of that trucker. *(Angry)* Are you comfortable, fella? I hope so! Because I'm not! Your keeping two diaries and fictionalizing events and dates was wonderful inspiration! Needless to say! But why?! Why, did you do it?! Your ego?! Because no one knows how to build a hazardous waste dump that works?! Because dump operators and politicians alike will all be gone in the thirty or fifty years it takes for the dump to start to leak?! Because the river already has a brilliant reddish-orange color?! Small risk! Big gains! You did all you could to protect us, fella! *(She notices an expression of pain on his face and rushes to comfort him.)*

BUSH: *(Speaking with a bit of difficulty)* Nita, don't be frightened. I'm alright. We're not surrounded yet. Luckily—-luckily, we're here in our trailer. Don't go away! Don't you love this land? The river nearby? The sky? Don't leave us!

NITA: *(Exasperated)* I'm not leaving. You should have seen me outwit the Environmental Protection Group! It wasn't easy under the circumstances. Waiting for that midnight knock on the door—so to speak!

BUSH: *(Gently)* When will my Evelyn be back?

NITA: Soon, Bush, soon.

BUSH: Evelyn was smiling at me when I gave her the earrings of gold and diamonds. I carried her over the threshold of our new home. She's not at peace with herself. No. She's a little stubborn sometimes. You know that too, Nita.

NITA: *(Not listening)* My workers know my rules are fair. It would be helpful for everyone concerned if there was general cooperation. Right?

BUSH: *(Enthused)* Right as rain!

NITA: *(Confidential tone)* Bush, don't let Evelyn get you down. She means well. *(Pause)* Concerning the suggested course of action for the business, the maintenance of reliability and trust is what counts. What is missing in all this are the facts. What will save our necks is that the diaries give different interpretations! My deepest fear is that we cannot compete by conventional methods. New strategies are necessary. Resources you can count on. Work hard and save. That used to be the secret. Today, it's not so simple.

BUSH: *(In a burst)* This trailer is a wall of windows! Why?! Why, did we set up our enterprise here!? People can look in the windows!

NITA: Bush, Bush, it's alright. What's going on in that head?

BUSH: Where's my wife Evelyn?!

NITA: She's home.

BUSH: Home. It takes just a fraction of a breath to say..."home". *(He starts to rise but falls back again into the chair.)* Nita, do you know that the human body is mostly salt water? And like the ocean...the tides affect us.

(Lights fade to blackness.)

END OF PLAY

www.ingramcontent.com/pod-product-compliance
Lightning Source LLC
Chambersburg PA
CBHW060543100426
42742CB00013B/2436